Beg to Differ

Joseph Agassi • Abraham Meidan

Beg to Differ

The Logic of Disputes and Argumentation

Copernicus Books is a brand of Springer

Joseph Agassi
Tel-Aviv University
Tel-Aviv, Israel

Abraham Meidan
WizSoft
Tel-Aviv, Israel

ISBN 978-3-319-33306-9   ISBN 978-3-319-33307-6   (eBook)
DOI 10.1007/978-3-319-33307-6

Library of Congress Control Number: 2016938794

© Springer International Publishing Switzerland 2016
This work is subject to copyright. All rights are reserved by the Publisher, whether the whole or part of the material is concerned, specifically the rights of translation, reprinting, reuse of illustrations, recitation, broadcasting, reproduction on microfilms or in any other physical way, and transmission or information storage and retrieval, electronic adaptation, computer software, or by similar or dissimilar methodology now known or hereafter developed.
The use of general descriptive names, registered names, trademarks, service marks, etc. in this publication does not imply, even in the absence of a specific statement, that such names are exempt from the relevant protective laws and regulations and therefore free for general use.
The publisher, the authors and the editors are safe to assume that the advice and information in this book are believed to be true and accurate at the date of publication. Neither the publisher nor the authors or the editors give a warranty, express or implied, with respect to the material contained herein or for any errors or omissions that may have been made.

Printed on acid-free paper

This Copernicus imprint is published by Springer Nature
The registered company is Springer International Publishing AG Switzerland

Preface

Most people get involved in arguments on some occasions or other. Unfortunately, many of these arguments are frustrating. How can this frustration be avoided? How should we conduct debates? These are the questions that the current handbook deals with.

Our basic assumption is that you can learn the rules of conducting debates so that you will enjoy them, and you will enjoy them mainly since you will learn from them, but you will also enjoy the game that you can view the way you view a game of chess.

Many other handbooks list suggestions as to how to conduct debates. Most of them refer to debates in the debating clubs that many schools have instituted. They list suggestions such as how you should look at your opponent, how you should dress and how you should talk in order to win the debate without losing friends. The present handbook does not belong to this genre. Our aim is to list the rules of debate that make the activity as rational as possible.

The suggestions we make here are not new. Rather, they describe the way rational debates are conducted in science. We suggest that implementing these rules in the debates that you have with your friends and relations will reduce the frustration and increase your ability to learn from them.

We will present our suggestions in two ways. The first few chapters present our views on rational debate, in contrast with the views that propel other handbooks. The next few chapters present the rules of rational debate. The following chapters review debates in various fields and discuss the relevance of the rules to the debates. We try there to review most of fields where popular debates take place.

The book addresses a wide audience—from students in secondary schools up to scholars in universities, from readers with theoretical interests to readers with practical ones. We assume no previous knowledge, so that everyone can read this book, yet we hope that our suggestions will interest and help everyone engaged in debates, including experts in the art of debates.

We hope that you find our suggestions practical and efficient. If not, please let us know, and tell us what is wrong with them. We thank you in advance for your criticism and promise to correct and improve our suggestions in the next edition of this handbook.

Tel-Aviv, Israel Joseph Agassi
Tel-Aviv, Israel Abraham Meidan
March 2015

Contents

1	**On the Frustration That Debates Cause**	1
	Avoiding Frustrating Debates	6
2	**Resolving a Dispute**	15
	Debates About Theories	21
3	**Improving the Wording of the Questions Under Dispute**	27
4	**The Burden of Proof**	41
	Generalizations and Existential Statements	42
5	**Disputes About General Facts and Theories**	45
	Ad-hoc Theories	47
	Simplicity	50
	Predictions vs. Explanations	52
	The Theory of Evolution or Evolutionism	55
	Global Warming	57
6	**Disputes About Statistical Generalizations**	59
	Accidental Patterns	66
	Debates About Healthy Diets	67
7	**Metaphysical Disputes**	69
	The Mind-Body Problem	71
	The Problem of Free Choice	75
	What Is Really the Case?	77
	Does God Exist?	78
8	**Disputes About History and Predictions**	83
	Long-Range Forecasts	89
	Global Famine	92

9	**Disputes About Technology, Including Medicine**	93
	Disputes About Advantages and Drawbacks	97
	Global Warming II	99
10	**Disputes About Ethics and Politics**	101
	The Choice of a Lifestyle	101
	Criteria for Ethics and Politics	102
	Politics	108
	Human Rights	110
	The Problem of Inequality	111
	National Rights	112
	Global Politics	113
	Popular Political Principles and Styles	114
11	**Disputes About Aesthetics**	117
12	**Conclusion**	123
	Appendix: Skepticism	127
	A Brief History of Skepticism	129
	Bibliography	133
	Index	135

Introduction

This handbook is an attempt to familiarize our readers in a very simple and easy manner the rule of the proper procedures of rational debate. The aim of this exercise is one: to reduce the frustration that many people experience when engaging in debates. The rationale for it is our opinion that the proper conduct of debates is both fun and great intellectual progress. It is an empirical observation that young people who did not do well in school become excellent students after spending some time in rabbinical schools, where they practice debates. If this is true, then it is but one illustration of the fact that learning to debate by the rules makes debate fun and debate is the fastest means for rapid progress in learning.

This then is a handbook on the theory and practice of argumentation. There are many kinds of argument, public and private, everyday, political and scientific. Their rules vary. We will touch upon this later on in some detail, but our chief concern is in the private debate between two individuals, dialogue (two-speak), including those dialogues that become public and engage public opinions. The paradigm cases of such arguments are those presented in the early dialogues of Plato and the published debates between the two greatest physicists of the twentieth century, Albert Einstein and Niels Bohr. Those latter concern the different ways of looking at quantum theory. And although today no physicist advocates the views of either Einstein or Bohr, the debate still is a classic.

A paragraph about Plato's early dialogues. They display the way to argue, and they are also our documentation about the rules of debate. Indeed, one may look at them as studies each devoted to a discussion of one rule. The leading character in these dialogues is Socrates, the greatest expert on argument ever. Yet he viewed the rules of the game as established and as well known. This does not mean that they are followed. Indeed, Plato's dialogues suggest very clearly that they were repeatedly violated. Plato, it seems, suggested that some experts—they were called sophists (*sophos* is wise)—taught aspiring politicians how to violate the rules of debates with impunity so as to win elections. Of course, cheating in every game is to be expected, and as we have today people who can teach how to cheat at cards or in business, there must have been such people in antiquity; yet Plato's sweeping charge against all the sophists is now doubted. He disagreed with them about the purpose of the game itself. He taught that proper dialogues end with proofs and they said proof is not attainable. The irony of the situation is that Plato's teacher, Socrates himself, was a sophist. To stress the sophist lesson that certain knowledge is unattainable he disclaimed the title of a sophist, to say he was not wise but aspired to be wise, he was not a sophist but a philosopher. (He invented this word.)

Though the rules of the game are known, their application is not unproblematic. One of the most important philosophical texts of the twentieth century is *The Logic of Scientific Discovery* by Karl Popper that presents science as a dialogue and the rules of dialogue as the rules of science. This handbook owes much to Plato and to Popper.

Now, speaking about scientific research, it is far from clear who plays the game; Einstein suggested once, rather humorously, that it is the game between the researcher and the Mother Nature. Some philosophers took this suggestion seriously and offered the view of science as such a game, not the game of dialogue but a game according to game theory. In this handbook we will not discuss game theory. And although we will not shun from discussing scientific research—in a manner that does not require of our reader to be in possession of special scientific knowledge—our concern is elsewhere. The case studies that we present here are more from familiar everyday situations, and for the reason that we have already mentioned. We want to influence your everyday conduct: we want to help you enrich your daily experiences by helping you develop proficiency at debating that will make you a friendly and helpful master of the art of debates. We offer many examples of common debates in the hope that some of them pertain to your experiences and that you will try to apply our suggestions, however tentatively and see whether they help you in your daily affairs, regardless of what occupation is or what your interests are, provided that they contain some intellectual component. We promise that this component will grow and to the benefit of both your intellectual and your social standing.

Tel-Aviv University	Joseph Agassi
Tel-Aviv, Israel	
WizSoft	Abraham Meidan
Tel-Aviv, Israel	
Spring 2015	

Chapter 1
On the Frustration That Debates Cause

Abstract In contemporary society disputes are usually considered frustrating and thus painful. This handbook advocates the opposite view: disputes can and should be fruitful and therefore enjoyable. Nevertheless, it is true: disputes can be frustrating. This book lists practical recommendations for rules that help avoid frustrating debates and construct fruitful ones.

All societies we know prefer agreement over disagreement. This leads to stagnation, of course, since a new idea is very likely to conflict with familiar ones. Yet the familiar ones are pleasant; they come with childhood memories, they come with mutual understanding and exchanging compliments around the tribal campfire. For, most societies are tribal; the most forceful feeling of belonging to the tribe is sharing values and all sorts of ideas that congeal into worldviews. The sense of tribal togetherness is the sense of distinctness, and distinctness comes easy with distinct myths and rituals. Thus, the distinction between us and them is through the difference in traditions that comprise myths and rituals.

Come to think of it, this is not exact: first we have a vague idea of the traditions of other tribes, and we know that we are right; as tribal traditions mature, some members of the tribe meet with traditions of other tribes, and the question rises seriously as to attitudes towards different traditions: first we know that we differ from them and of course we are right, and then, as we learn more about their traditions, we face seriously the question, who is right, we or they? We then compare traditional myths and find that they are not so different. Thus, Ishtar is Esther, is Aphrodite, is Venus.

Come to think of it, this is not surprising. All these goddesses are symbols for beauty, and beauty is one. What may be different is ideas about the nature of things; some tribe has more knowledge about sticks and some are better informed of stones. This hardly makes a difference between tribes: when one tribe can learn something from another tribe, there can hardly be objection to their doing so. Some myths conflict with each other, or at least seem to. For example, how many elements are there? The Greeks say, four; the Chinese say five. We can reconcile these two views. On the whole, it is ancient knowledge that any two conflicting ideas can be reconciled with each other. This is hard to believe, and perhaps it is an exaggeration. This matters little here, since this handbook does not address this issue; rather, it concerns with disputes, and more so with the pleasure of disagreement. The idea that conflicting view can be reconciled is an example of an expression of dislike of disagreement. This dislike is a concern of the present study, since we aim to show why people dislike disputes and help them develop a taste for it.

Tribalism, to repeat, is a major cause for the preference for agreement over disagreement, which is the preference for association with relatives over association with strangers. This preference enhances both agreement with relatives and disagreement with strangers. These agreement and disagreement refer to myth and rituals. As to myths, they are usually reconciled; this leads to a stress of rituals, especially taboos: one tribe does not consume fish and another tribe does not consume foul. The great Greek historian Herodotus reported that Persians were shocked to learn that Greeks bury their dead as Greeks were equally shocked to learn that Persians leave the copses of their dead on mountaintops for birds to consume.

We will not discuss customs here, religious or social. Rather, we will stress that these changes, and often out of disagreements about them and criticisms of them that with public support. These criticisms usually meet with hostility; even people who launch them or who finally admit them, do so distastefully. We think the distaste is harmful: it makes necessary change come less often and less frequently than is desirable. To repeat, they belong to our tribal past. We are far less tribal these days; most of us befriend people and prefer their company and cooperation that to that of relatives. Indeed, we teach our children to call our friends uncles and aunts. We cannot easily befriend people who condone murder, but we find it easy to befriend people who vote for different parties than we do. So we have to learn to see that debates with them can be fun, and should be fun if we learn from debates, since learning is fun. The greatest philosopher of all times, Plato, repeatedly spoke in favor of disputes (despite his having advocated a tribal society). He said, consider error as illness and criticism as cure; we hate illness and we may dislike the bitterness of the medication, but we do not hate medication.

In modern society, we face disagreement daily on various issues, from the smallest to the largest; we often argue with people with whom we disagree. Some people prefer to disagree about matters that matter very little, that they agree about their worthlessness: presumably they do so in order to avoid serious debates. Presumably they prefer not to risk losing their faith in what they think matters, and so they prefer not to face criticism of their views on what matters and so they prefer to argue about what they think does not matter. Clearly, this is ostrich policy. If their opinions signify, then they should care to ask, are these opinions true? For this they would wish to hear the most severe criticism of their opinions in the hope to be able to rebuff them; if their serious views are erroneous and if they are serious about them, then they would love to be corrected. All this is opaque: what is valid criticism? How can it be rebuffed? How does one change one's view as a result of criticism? We will come to this in great detail soon enough.

Serious people usually do not argue about small matters as they are not worth the time and effort, and they do not argue about the biggest potentially unsolvable matters, for the same reason. Indeed, we can say, this is precisely what makes people serious: one is serious if and only if one takes one's opinions seriously and examines them seriously. Serious opinions are answers to serious questions, then, but not the other way around: some serious issues are not fit to argue about. What issues are fit to argue about? On this question we have no generally accepted rules, and hardly anyone cares to give this question serious, conscious consideration and offer a rule for possible general adoption. Of course, the question pertains both to public and to individual opinions and conduct. People in different circumstances decide differently about what is fit for debate and what not. Publicly, the matter is more important and still hardly governed by any rule: leading thinkers who have to decide on such matters usually follow custom or else they do so on the spur-of-the-moment. So do parliamentary committees as they discuss what to put on the public agenda for debate. So do journalists, or rather editors of newspapers and periodicals. These leading thinkers must decide quickly whether it is worthwhile to argue about particular questions in public or only with some specific people (friends, relatives, peers or business associates). On any disagreement it is easy to find reasons for arguing about it and reasons for not arguing about it; and when arguing, there are reasons for terminating the argument or for continuing to debate the issue—unless one party gives in to the other, thereby concluding the debate, of course. No clear rules exist. High-school debating society coaches, for example, set guidelines. Some coaches advise to never admit error; others say that there is no value to debates unless both parties are ready to admit error honestly and say openly that they are unfamiliar with a point made by the opponent and to concede when they consider themselves defeated or agree the possibility that they have lost when this is how the situation looks to them but they feel the need to sleep on it.

All this holds for all debates, public or private; in private, having offered a deadly argument, one may desist from arguing for fear of offending the opponent and one may insist that the opponent should openly admit defeat. Clearly, people usually feel offended when they lose a debate and outraged when forced to admit this openly. This is a shame. To repeat, Plato stressed this a few times: people can gain from debates even (or *particularly*) when they lose, since they can learn where they were in error and avoid such errors in the future. This trial-and-error is a very important way of learning. While many teachers do not like to admit it, trial and error beats learning by rote any day, as ample psychological experiments show.

To repeat, most people take it for granted that agreement may be hard to come by, but that it is always preferable to disagreement. This view has many expressions. In particular, we are told that collaboration requires agreement. This is not always so: in tribal societies collaboration requires agreement; in modern societies collaboration requires a shared interest. Normally, in modern societies parties to ventures put aside their opinions and favor compromises. We will return to this soon. For now, let us register our disagreement with the view that agreement is harder to reach than disagreement and with the view that agreement is superior to disagreement. We claim that it is easy to follow received opinions, and hard to criticize them, yet this is often a worthwhile activity, since we can often learn from criticism and lead to the improvement of public opinion and to diverse applications. It is particularly easy to achieve agreement if we are not particularly interested in the *truth*: we then say, all right, have it your way. At times, agreement clearly seems to be most desirable: for example, when asking, "Will you marry me?" Of course, the answer, "yes, I will" is greatly desired. The reason for this seems to be simple, but, as anyone who watches soap operas knows, it is far from simple. "Will you marry me?" combines a few questions, two samples of which are predominant: first, do you want to share live with me, share property with me, have children with me, and so on? And second, do you consider it wise for us to do this now? The first set of questions has either an obvious answer, or one that is too complicated. Let us skip it. The second is very important, always open to rational deliberations, and so it is always wise to debate it before deciding on it. For example, even on the supposition that two individuals are passionately in love with each other, there are many ways to act on this supposition. So the question is: which way is the most advisable for us here and now? This question involves a preliminary debate on the arguments for and against any option, followed by a debate over the initial question: is it wise for the two to get married in the near future? Moreover, the more liberal a society, the more options the couple face to choose from. In particular, today the choice between civil and religious marriage, civil marriage, or cohabitation. (When the liberal philosopher Bertrand Russell mentioned the option of premarital sex and of cohabitation he disqualified himself from teaching in a New York college, which is unthinkable today.) To return to our initial point, the preference in asking the initial question, "Will you marry me?" is for an immediate affirmative response that does not require a prior debate about it.

The fact remains: most people in modern society find argument painful. They find agreement agreeable and disagreement disagreeable. Why is this the case? More important, how can we alter it? Many possible explanations for the fact are available; one of these is so paramount that we may ignore the others: cooperation is essential, and agreement is considered essential for cooperation. Admittedly, cooperation is essential; yet agreement is *not* essential for it. Moreover, debate comprises a form of cooperation, and decisions reached following a debate (on an issue regarding which significant disagreement exists) yields better cooperation than decision reached otherwise, say in accord with the opinion of the senior party. The debate itself may also eliminate significant errors that may threaten the cooperation. Cooperating parties may find that they disagree, at times even on central issues; but then, debate may lead to compromise or to one of them granting the other the benefit of the doubt. Thus, cooperation also evolves through debate. Of course, during the process, one party may die (for example, if the party is a patient and the debate concerns treatment), but the cooperation can continue: debate is impersonal. At times, the disagreement is too deep and the cooperation stops or perhaps is avoided in the first place. Would it be better to continue cooperating despite the disagreement, or would it have been preferable had the disagreement not appeared in the first place? Clearly, there is no general answer to this question; in certain instances, it is better to cooperate despite disagreement and in others not. In particular, when cooperation must continue, say in the case of allies fighting a war, then wise parties do postpone the debate for the day after victory is achieved. In contrast, when parties consider whether they should wage a war against one another, then, clearly, agreement is preferable regarding whether all alternatives to war have been tried and failed despite arduous efforts.

Consider divorce proper. It is sad, to be sure. This does not mean that the divorce is bad: it may be and it often is the best solution of a difficult problem. What is obvious though, is that marriage not well thought out is more likely to lead to divorce than a well thought-out marriage, especially since serious thinking may prevent ill-conceived marriages. Many people find distasteful serious deliberations about marriage, no matter how serious they may be. Those who consider marriage a responsible decision will disagree and will allow that they should debate this matter before making the decision. They may then agree but admit that the debate itself is unpleasant. We wish to discover the reason for this and we wish to show that it can be pleasant even if it leads to a heartbreaking decision to postpone or avoid marriage.

Nevertheless, the psychological fact remains: many people suffer from a sense of humiliation when they lose a debate. That this is so when their wish to get married is frustrated is obvious. But this is true even when the debate is abstract and with no obvious consequences for the losing party: the loss of the debate in itself hurts. Why? Even when there are no immediate personal consequences to the loss, the loss seems a humiliation for both psychological causes and for intellectual reasons. Listing and examining the psychological causes is beyond the scope of this handbook. We can offer some intellectual reasons and discuss them; this should help us offer some guidelines, however, regarding how to avoid (or at least minimize) this pain, and even replace it with the pleasure of learning. First, be aware of this psychological phenomenon. As psychologists have repeatedly discovered, awareness of an irrational psychological disposition reduces it. Second, try repeatedly to make the debate as impersonal as possible. Instead of arguing about personal issues, argue about general ideas, perhaps also change sides with your opponent: as they often say, things look differently from different positions, and thus it is worthwhile to see how it looks from over there.

It is difficult to exaggerate the importance of this move. All too often we are not aware of the feelings of people whose role we have never shared and we are even more often ignorant of how the world looks from the viewpoint of the other. At times all that we need to broaden our view is to try: we often reverse roles unawares; think of a near-accident on the road and of the two involved drivers who are self-righteously angry with each other. They may try to remember such near-accidents when they played the opposite role. At times this is very different. Think of the effort it took experimental psychologists to convince jailers to change place with prisoners for a day or two. The outcome surprised them all, including the psychologists.

We are all fallible: we all make mistakes, and when others draw our attention to our mistakes they are doing us a favor. True, some mistakes are silly and so having made them may reasonably be downright embarrassing, and people may be highly annoyed at having made them. They are then apt to project (in Freudian terminology) this annoyance at the ones who point out their mistakes. This is the well-known phenomenon of shooting the messenger. Some people are even annoyed at their own fallibility. They are at liberty to feel that way, but they should not blame others for it. Being sick is bad; yet, since being informed of our sickness is preferable to staying ignorant about it, we condemn blaming physicians who convey bad news.

Avoiding Frustrating Debates

Disagreements, disputes, debates, arguments, and confrontations are quite common in modern society. Regrettably, they are all too often quite futile as well: differing parties stick to their guns, refuse to learn anything from each other, and end with ill feelings and frustration. The possible reasons for the displeasure with these are many, but we will here center mainly on one: the frustration that accompanies them. We do so for two reasons: first, it is the cardinal reason and overcoming it is a tremendous relief, and second, it is the easiest to remedy and in the most interesting manner to boot.

No matter how unpleasant confrontations are, no matter how much forethought and energy and restraint we invest in efforts to avoid them, too often we fail. Often, problems under dispute beg for resolutions, and so repressed disputes over them repeatedly reemerge and finally burst into full confrontations that soon lead to regret and resolution to be more restrained. To no avail. This experience is then repeated. The repeated experience is naturally increasingly frustrating as they indicate some deep-seated sense of helplessness. Frustration deepens the ill feeling. The deep ill feelings make it ever harder to avoid future confrontations and so on. This process can terminate in death or in a radical change: transfer of one party to another location, a breakup of a partnership, a divorce. Divorce may be a part of the process, however. Think of actors Robert Wagner and Natalie Wood who married and divorced and remarried.

Clearly, the more civilized a confrontation is, that is, the more it is an exchange of opinions, the less frustrating it may be. Yet, however civilized an exchange of opinions may be, the parties to it are likely to still feel deep down inside that the source of the confrontation is ugly—an expression of unfriendly, aggressive feelings towards opponents, towards people who reject significant and obviously true opinions on some important matter.

At times this is inevitable. Many a divorce came about after one party to a marriage discovered a nasty streak in the other party that they could not remove by some reproof as it rests on some prejudice. The prejudice may be political. The divorce may be the result of one party holding progressive political views that the other party finds too naïve as the other party holds reactionary opinions that the one party finds cruel. We have already expressed our opinion about such divorces: they indicate that the couples in question got married too soon and not responsibly: people should know each other well enough when they get married to avoid finding their partner's political views after marriage. Yet many young people in love care too little about politics to imagine that political disagreements can break their marriages. And they are usually right: if any political disagreement were the cause of a divorce, then most marriages would not hold as well as they do. But disagreements between a partner who supports democracy and a partner who considers this naïve is a different matter altogether.

Such cases are scarce, if only because hostility to democracy is rare in contemporary society and democracy recommends debates on principle. As experience repeatedly illustrates, the possibility of useful debates is what makes disagreements between spouses no threat to the stability of their marriage. We would go further and declare it a good means for the fusion of the parties into a stable marriage. Civilized debates may be fruitful and fruitful debates raise a sense of gratitude, as they prevent some embarrassing and dangerous errors. Admittedly, such debates, no matter how useful they are, may very well combine with some personal animosity (covert or even overt; even in the family). Yet ultimately debate, however unpleasant it may be, prevents embarrassment and dangerous error. Even if the error is not dangerous, even when it is common, the recognition that the debate has eradicated it may be exhilarating. And indeed, personal animosity (no matter how intense) can give way to a sense of pleasure as frustration gives way to a sense of benefit from debates; for, learning is always a source of great pleasure. Indeed, many philosophers go as far as to say that all learning involves criticism of diverse answers to diverse questions, including previously unimagined wild answers and previously unimagined arguments against them.

The philosophers who go as far as to say that all learning involves criticism are aware of the fact that this sounds strange. Think of a person who is ignorant of modern science and of the modern gadgets that surround us in the modern world and that would be impossible but for the advancement in science. Is their ignorance due to error? Which error? Let us go further and consider magically-minded people. It is hard to see their ignorance as rooted in error. When pre-literate people come in touch with the modern world, they may see airplanes descend from the blue sky and people emerge from them. They are deeply impressed and they view it as powerful magic. It is hard to judge whether this experience clashes with any opinion they have, and it is hard to see that the new impressive experience teaches them anything about the world. By contrast, consider the civilized people who saw airplanes for the first time as the Wright brothers succeeded in building flying machines. They were surprised because they held firmly the opinion that people cannot fly. Particularly experts, such as professors of physics, were of the opinion that the Wright brothers criticized effectively. The experts who knew about flights of birds and of kites and of people who flew on kites—that are called gliders—were particularly clear about the impossibility of flying machines—airplanes. They learned a lot from the success of the Wright brothers to fly on kites propelled by engines. This, however is an aside that we will not pursue, since the present study concerns all sorts of confrontations, not ones that are specific to science and to scientific technology. People whose daily work is scientific, theoretical or technological, have sophisticated attitudes to confrontations that require separate treatments.

Our claim is that debate is fruitful, then, rests on our claim that criticism is useful. Who needs criticism, asked leading science-fiction writer James Blish. Everybody, he answered his own question. Why then is debate so often futile? Why then does it so often end up with nothing but a strong, annoying sense of frustration?

Part of the answer is psychological, which, to repeat, lies beyond the realm of this handbook. But the answer is not all psychological: part of it is that successful debate is rare. Notably, this is a pity, particularly since debate is not very costly in terms of time and effort investment; on the contrary, as we have observed, it is frequently unavoidable; and when properly conducted, it is often so beneficial as to be highly cost-effective. Of course, when we say that debate is wonderful and dismiss evidence to the contrary as due to defective performance, our conduct may be dogmatic, and our dismissal of the evidence to the contrary may be mere defensiveness. This is particularly so when evidence to the contrary is dismissed simply because it is evidence to the contrary. Thus, when dogmatists fail in their effort to convince their neighbors and they dismiss these neighbors as inept, they are likely to use the fact that they have failed to convince their neighbors as sufficient evidence that they are inept. Even so, in this case our dogmatist must admit error: the effort to convince people whom it is impossible to convince rests on error, on the ignorance of their ineptness. Usually, our dogmatist refuses to admit even this error: effort to convince them is giving them the benefit of the doubt. We hope that the present handbook never uses this kind of argument. First, this handbook is written not in efforts to convince but in effort to help people improve. We address people whom confrontations frustrate and who are unable to overcome the frustration; we tell you that you are able to overcome the frustration and we offer simple exercises that will satisfy you. If not, then we are in error, and if you will be kind enough to write to us, then we will try to take account of your criticism and complaint and improve this handbook.

Thinkers of the Age of Reason (the seventeenth century and more so the eighteenth century) regularly repeated the broadly consensual slogan that debates should cease rapidly, that at best only their first bouts may yield some benefit, and that afterwards they cost more than they are worth: at first they may enlighten, but soon they produce more heat than light. There is much wisdom in this view that was common in the Age of Reason: it is wise to avoid engaging in an activity that results in frustration, and if the first round or two did not bear fruit, then it is unwise to continue since the opponents may be too dogmatic to be willing to learn. But some debates are very fruitful, and usually we cannot know in advance which debate is going to be fruitful. This renders debate a kind of wild gold rush: regardless of how frustrated prospectors usually are, they still go on searching in the hope of hitting a goldmine.

This sounds as if prospectors do not learn from criticism. And indeed, some prospectors do not. Usually, they test some hunches and as a result of frustration they may give up the hunches—about kinds of promising locations or about kinds of prospecting methods or anything else. If they have no hunches, then there is little for experience that they can use as criticism.

Indeed, the same assumption that a gold rush may succeed drives some people to wild prospecting; it drives others to study the matter and seek some ideas that will improve their odds. This tendency leads to organized prospecting, without totally eliminating wild prospecting. Wild prospectors may of course wish to benefit from the knowledge available to the organized prospectors, but they may be unaware of their existence, have no access to their knowledge base, or simply distrust whatever the organized prospectors consider reliable knowledge and prefer their own gut feelings. The same holds true for debates: knowledge is scarce regarding which debates are less frustrating and more promising.

We may take this example a step further. Prospectors, even lone ones, may benefit from a good theory that will improve their odds. If the thinkers of the Age of Reason were right in their assumption that debate produce more heat than light and that thereby it creates more risks than opportunities, then in search for increased efficiency we should seek cold debate akin to cold light. Alternatively, we may seek unregistered, unexpected prospecting opportunities. What usually causes debate to heat up is frustration. What then raises frustration in debate? This is a question that we will discuss here at length. We aim to advise our readers and help them train themselves in the art of debates, rendering debates more pleasant and hopefully more fruitful and decidedly less frustrating.

Still, this we can say right off the bat. Frustration is due to the gap between expectation and achievement. We can see this in some simple experiments. Consider this example. When we get stuck in a traffic jam we are frustrated and we blame the traffic jam. This is an error, and even an easily correctable one. For suppose you know that you are going to pump into a traffic jam; suppose you know that this is a possibility and you take the chance; the traffic jam then will frustrate you much less, if at all. You may be well prepared for it and then find it amusing. The difference between the prepared and the unprepared is the same as the difference between the young, impatient prospector and the well-trained old one. Of course, after sufficient frustration, most young prospectors leave if they can to seek their fortunes elsewhere. To repeat, many people who try to avoid confrontations fail to do so. And then they still expect to have the next one more fruitful. And so, the frustration from confrontations is due to the hope that they will bear fruit. Even if you will learn nothing more from the present handbook, this you should learn right now and benefit from it at once: unless you have reason to expect the next confrontation to be less frustrating than earlier ones and if all the same you cannot avoid it, then at the very least do not expect that it will not frustrate you yet again. But, of course, we promise you right now that we will offer you ample reason to expect the next confrontation you will come across to be much less frustrating and hopefully even to expect that you will enjoy it. How can we promise this? Let us answer this question right away. For, we have no secret and we pull no rabbit out of top hats. On the contrary, the technique that we will help you acquire is ancient.

We take as our default hypothesis the following assertions. The extant rules of debating procedure can render debates efficient to a sufficient extent that they merit efforts to study and to master. Also, that the observed futility of debates is all too often the result of poor attention to these available procedures. One more assertion: These techniques are quite easy to master. They are straightforward and hold for a number of public and private activities. Many people try their hands at writing—poetry, stories, novels, scientific papers, scientific monographs or textbooks—and are met with an increasing sense of frustration simply because they do not know that there are rules to master that help avoid frustration. This is why new books regularly appear and schools regularly open with the promise of offering training in various skills and vocations. Training imparts skills; this does not assure success, but it normally does reduce the sense of frustration. People purchase handbooks and register in training programs with the hope of acquiring these skills. At times the outcome is felicitous, at times not; some give up, and some keep trying. This is sheer commonsense, yet repeatedly people ignore the need to acquire the necessary skills, often being unaware of the basic need for them. Thus, many young people try their hands in writing poetry with no idea that this discipline can be learned. This is all the more so with debates. There is nothing inherent to debating skills. In ancient Athens, people commonly appreciated that debates require skill, and renowned experts (known as sophists, namely wise people) taught these skills for fees.

The most obvious case of frustration is poetry. Most people take it for granted that there is no need to acquire any skill to write poems. This idea gains very strong support from the fact that some of the greatest poets were born poets. This is true of all skills. It sounds incredible that some people are born pianists or born car-drivers. But this is an attested fact. And it is an attested fact that poetry is a skill that one can acquire. Young people who write poems with no training usually write worthless pieces and only if they receive criticism they either get frustrated and cease writing or try to acquire the necessary skills. Yet skills are usually necessary, but seldom sufficient. They are sufficient to remove the normal frustrations of the unskilled, but more cannot be promised. We stress this repeatedly: of course, in every art there are those who are born experts, who received no training but show remarkable abilities and are highly productive. This phenomenon leads many to the false opinion that learning any craft is useless: either you are born gifted or not. This is rather silly, since most of the proficient in most fields have studied in some manner and acquired their skills. Naturally, the same goes for the art of argumentation.

And, just as people find it easy to write poems and are frustrated if they do not acquire some skill at it, so people find it easy to engage in confrontation and are frustrated if they do not acquire some skill at it. Yet it is not always easy to tell budding poets effectively that they may benefit from the acquisition of skills that is hardly problematic.

So do read this book as a handbook, as a training manual in the art of argumentation and see if it increases your debating skill and reduces your sense of frustration when debating or not. You should not be too patient with us and you need not go far: you can test our claim that we are helpful almost at once. You should benefit from our advice almost instantaneously in that it should reduce your sense of frustration almost at once. We hope that you will find that application of our proposals will reduce your sense of frustration considerably and increase the sense of fun from debates that you participate in.

We seek to help people master the rules of proper debate, and with ease. As discussed above, such learning will not assure success to all readers in every debate, but it will enable readers' experience with debate to become much less frustrating and much more rewarding, and almost at once.

Admittedly, let us repeat, the appeal to cautious optimism is often the unfair fending off complaints about failure. Let us specify: the excuse that failure is rare is statistical and so it is hard to refute. This excuse may pacify the complaining party by shifting the blame from the proposal to some rare ill luck (not to mention some nastier excuses, such as accusation of those who complain for some defect or ill will). But then, as complaints accumulate and reports of success falter, cautious optimism gives way to despair. We will see to it that this will not be the case regarding our cautious optimism here. Our discussion of the efficient procedure for managing disputes, for presenting arguments, and for helping to render this a standard procedure, though cautiously optimist, is meant to serve as a tool for the alteration of public standards—no less! Finally, to repeat, any criticism of our errors we will welcome and try to improve our advice.

The procedures we advocate have been adopted in diverse kinds of instances with tremendous success. The most obvious examples are debates in scientific circles, in legislatures, and in law courts. Some debates have prevented wars, especially civil wars (since it is easier to argue with siblings than with strangers). Our aim is to integrate practices from these fields into everyday life: we focus less on innovation and more on popularization.

In this regard, we take as our starting point the familiar though oddly ignored observation about differences between diverse societies regarding the sense of frustration. It is no secret that in some societies—both traditional and modern—the sense of frustration from debates is either maximal or minimal, simply because of the different approach different cultures take to disagreement. Individuals experience higher or lower levels of frustration from debates as a function of the broader social perspective regarding debates.

In most modern societies, debate is usually a familiar occurrence; some societies have outlawed and penalized debate, with the police imposing the ban strictly—they are known as dictatorships. Indeed, some scholars suggest that negative attitude towards fruitful discourse is what makes a regime dictatorial. Consequently, these scholars hardly distinguish between Fascist and Communist regimes. Others find this characterization offensive, as they may be friendly to the Communist ideals and thus even more hostile to the Fascist ones than their democratic colleagues, and so they dispute the notion that the (admittedly regrettable) ban on debate in Communist regimes renders Communism as objectionable as Fascism. Some such scholars even go so far as to differentiate between a ban on debates for legitimate and illegitimate reasons. Their democratic colleagues, however, are not lost for an answer: they say, the road to hell is paved with good intentions, and debate is the best means for stopping us from taking that road. They say, what makes decent Communist leaders dictators is the Communist ban on debate. Even if the ban is on some sort of debate, there is an urgent need to debate this very ban. This is a general truth: debate is the best known means for revealing the mistaken judging appraising dangerous moves as good measures. The sympathizers with Communism may respond by drawing attention to circumstances that impose limitation on debate. Needless to say, this debate about the usefulness of debate (this meta-debate, as philosophers would say) is very frustrating. We therefore stop following it here, at least for a while. We will discuss later the ways to render it very fruitful and fun.

Some traditional societies explicitly proscribe debate, although not necessarily politically and so with no police force imposing the ban; they merely consider it bad manners and often declare it religiously or socially detrimental. Notably, in all societies, even in relatively modern ones, magic is still widespread simply because sufficiently many people consider it very rude to argue against current magical practices. In traditional China and Japan, the customary sensitivity regarding embarrassment is so great that the tradition discourages asking a question that might remain unanswered or raise controversy, and it encourages answering a question in the manner that will please those who are so insensitive as to ask that very question. The cultural tendency to avoid debates creates a communication barrier that is so tremendous as to be scarcely surmountable: any attempt to question this tradition is conceived as an act of questioning tradition as such, which tradition naturally proscribes. The situation can be even worse: to be efficient, debate about manners requires some knowledge about manners, yet societies such as the traditional Chinese consider it bad manners to inquire about manners. This forces people to try to decipher what the customary manners are. This is a most frustrating situation, and pondering on it will explain why in the West, the practice of debating persists despite all the enormous frustrations that it brings in its wake and despite great efforts to block it: the absence of debate is even more frustrating. The knowledge of this fact—that the suppression of debates is more frustrating than the participation in debates—is thus already a factor that may reduce the frustration of debates.

This then is our central point: *efforts at reducing the frustration that debates cause by seeking to avoid debate is useless; there are better and more efficient ways to reduce the frustration that debates cause.*

So much for societies that place this or that sort of restriction on debates. Let us then move to enclaves in Western societies in which on the whole debates are commonly admitted and their presence does not cause as much frustration as in more traditional parts of these societies. The first example that comes to mind is traditional scholastic or Talmudic disputations and their derivatives usually known by the general name of casuistry. Strangely, casuists never found the futility of their debates frustrating. This has an important and enlightening explanation: the futility of debates did not frustrate them because they saw in them a religious value, and an assured value at that. Moreover, they took it for granted that other than religious value, debates have little value; moreover, as we have already observed, (quite generally) a low expectation come with a low level of frustration, since frustration is due to unfulfilled expectations.

Casuistry is of course beyond the scope of this handbook and we mention it here only as an enclave of standard disputations and as a case of low expectations that prevent a high sense of frustration. Unrealistic expectations from debates and their resultant frustrations are evident, for example, in cases of arguments conducted in the hope of swaying the political opinions of peers rapidly—say, in one prolonged discussion—especially on the eve of some important elections. The high expectation often persists although the matters in question are subject to ongoing debates over the course of generations by wise scholars and politicians, with no conclusion in sight. This situation raises the question, why do people who habitually engage in political disputes not learn from their own experiences? Why do they not learn to lower their expectations? The answer is that they take their views as obviously true and so they ascribe unreasonableness to their peers' disagreements with them. Since they know their peers to be eminently reasonable, they may repeatedly expect that they will be able to show their peers quickly what oversight leads to their dissent, and thereby destroy it. And such cases do occur (see below), and they are impressive, no matter how rare they are. The trouble is that all too often all sides to a political debate share this expectation, so that each expects opponents to capitulate fast, which of course is impossible. The parties remain puzzled but see no other course but to retry. This mounts frustration. This leads to despair rather than to efforts to modify expectations.

The crux of this situation, let us repeat, is that all sides to a dispute are intelligent and each finds the opinions of the others unintelligent. The obvious fact is that we are all fallible and that therefore the view of our friends as intelligent should not lead us to the conclusion that they are usually right and their dissent form us on the point at the present issue is an exception. Rather, it is the paucity of intelligent thinking that makes us all so much in agreement with our friends.

Hence, we should not always expect debates to be fruitless. On the contrary, we will later discuss casuist debates and explain what imposes futility on them, so that those who wish to avoid futility (our intended readers) will know how to do so. Such knowledge will not assure success, but it will prevent assured failure. That is to say, the conduct that causes failure can often be found and avoided, by a sort of mental hygiene—the sort of mental hygiene that we recommend. Indeed, much of what we hope to impart to our readers are some simple rules of mental hygiene that with little effort will reduce frustration drastically. (The best medicine, we know, is preventive medicine. Indeed, modern medicine began in the middle of the nineteenth century (or a few bit later) with (or soon after) the discovery of preventive medicine that was more efficient than was known before. But even traditional medicine was largely preventive, such as quarantine of the sick, which is ancient. In debate, by the way, avoiding entering debates with casuists is the parallel to this, and a very good method indeed. This raises the question, what is the best method for identifying the casuist? We will answer this question later in some detail.)

Clearly, not all debates are fruitless. For one thing, fortunately, some debates can end in quick conclusion, regardless of the parties' debating skills. An obvious example of this type of resolution can involve the deadline imposed on newspaper editors by default: not deciding to print an item by the print deadline amounts to deciding to reject it. Hence, the debates that go on regularly in newspapers editorial boards are never futile although they can frustrate the journalists whose contributions are always rejected. Thus, dramas, movies, or TV series that deal with the press often appear as immensely frustrating for the struggling hero the young or dissident journalist. Such frustrations are inevitable, and we cannot hope to eliminate them; we can only hope to reduce them to a reasonable level. Another example is from the world of commerce, which also offers a plenty of instances of deadlines. Every time that outside factors impose a deadline on a commercial firm, members of that firm must curb debate, since leaving it open forces the deadline to close it by default. It is always wise to accept the decision that a deadline imposes some time before it arrives, when the deadline is near enough for those who should abide by it to realize that soon the time is up. And, of course, the most obvious deadline is any lull before a storm, including the quiet before a battle.

This is equally true of time-restricted court cases. In law courts, the rules of debates are usually entrenched just in order to prevent delay in reaching decision. In courts, presentations of disputes and arguments follow a relatively clear procedure, largely determined by the laws of evidence. Obviously, these procedures are largely artificial and thus not always applicable even in courts, so that mistrials are unavoidable. Court procedures balance the cost caused by the waste of time against the cost of handling such cases. In particular, there are strict laws as to the possibility of reopening a trial. It follows that court procedures are seldom applicable to regular out-of-court disputes or even to mere arbitrations. Yet they may serve as evidence that supports the hope that the use of proper procedure will reduce frustration considerably, in order to make it reasonable. (Talmudic legal procedures as practiced in traditional Jewish law courts ignore deadlines as much as possible and spare no time in efforts to go to the roots of problems. There is no pretense at practicality there, even though there is hope that a deep examination will produce a reasonable precedent.)

Let us make an additional observation about court procedure. Even when that procedure is not fully determined, the system expects judges to fill gaps and supply missing details with the aid of sheer common sense. (Indeed, at times judges are encourages to prefer commonsense to a law and thus create a significant precedent.) We propose, therefore, that without the use of the laws of evidence, and with no help from any judge, parties to any dispute should use their common sense and agree on a reasonable procedure, thus increasing the chances of alleviating frustration. This eliminates the need for judges—at the cost of the parties to the debate acquiring some competence.

The first point of procedure that we propose, then, is this. Whenever a dispute begins to frustrate, the disputing parties should consider the option of taking a break in the discussion in order to examine the procedure that they were following and to return to the debate, if at all, only after having cleared matters and agreed between themselves about a decision on a procedure that may hopefully reduce frustration somewhat. Even if that decision is erroneous, it need not frustrate, as they may repeat the process as much as they judge necessary. Also, they may find the procedure we propose interesting. Even when all efforts at rethinking procedure fail, the result need not frustrate, as it will guide the parties to the debate to terminate it instead.

Chapter 2
Resolving a Dispute

Abstract Do not try to resolve disputes by measuring objectively the plausibility of the opinions under dispute. Very plausibly, no objective measure exists for the plausibility of statements.

In this chapter we offer a review of some suggestions that popular teachers of argumentation offer as the best methods for resolving disputes. Let us say at once, most of the methods that popular advisers offer we reject right off the bat. We offer, instead, the very best methods that the best experts use, among them top scientific researchers, lawyers, even philosophers. When we learn a skill, we do not use instruments that differ from those that the best experts use. True, some parents play chess with their young offspring in a manner different form the manner they play with adults: they usually begin with taking off the chessboard one of their pieces, usually their right rook. This insures that their offspring will have great difficulty adjusting to the normal chessboard. The matter differs with child violinists: they use small violins simply because the usual size ones are too big for them to hold. They get normal size ones as soon as they can hold them. In computer courses a custom developed of teaching beginners out-of-date program languages that were supposed to be simple and so preferable. Fortunately, this custom stopped. In other courses teachers often use tools for beginners that are different from those that experts use. We find this deplorable. We offer in this handbook nothing but the very best.

First, some popular teachers of argumentation have suggested that disputes may be resolved by a successful search for some statements upon which the differing parties may be in agreement so as to build on it a case that will not be under dispute so that it will replace the disputed option or options. At times, however rarely, the parties to the dispute may agree to proceed on the supposition that they do agree about some statement that can lead to some relief and see how it evolves. It then will transpire that the statement will not lead to results that all parties will agree upon, so that the discussion would be sheer waste of time. It will be very unlikely that the agreed-upon statement will lead to statements that all parties will agree about and thus have the dispute resolved. It most likely, almost inevitably, turn out to tip the scale in favor of one of the parties in the dispute. And then, naturally, the other party will recognize it and withdraw its initial agreement. To avoid this, the statement that the parties should agree upon before the debate starts may express some middle position that the disputants could possibly reach at the end of the debate. This method seldom works, since in many cases such statements are unavailable, whether in principle or in practice. When the dispute is theoretical, it is a matter of principle rather than of interest, so that *a priori* a compromise is silly. A compromise makes sense when the dispute concerns some advantage that the disputing parties seek. When the parties go for one object of their desire, say a rare work of art, clearly a compromise is less obvious an option than when it is financial asset. Even then, when it is linked to control over a financial firm, things get harder to get compromise about. In many cases, both extremes are obviously superior to a compromise—if it exists in the first place. We have already referred to the idea that is well known in economics, as there are examples in that field of cases where the best is not available and the second best is not the option nearest to the best. The very suggestion that there is a statement—for the disputing parties to seek—that will dissipate the dispute, shows that the dispute is not serious and that the disputing parties aim at a compromise. Even then, however, resolution is not easy, as parties to a dispute may cling to some relevant views—dogmatically or rationally: even if the statement that should resolve the dispute is available, noticing that endorsing that statement amounts to the admission of defeat may very well make any party to a dispute reject it rather than admit defeat.

A view that some popular teachers of argumentation suggest is that of resolving disputes looks more serious. Indeed, it is popular among philosophy professors. We will argue that it seems realistic but it is the very opposite, and the philosophers engaged in it do not mean to offer it as a practical advice, although many of their fans misunderstand them to mean that. The advice is to resolve all disputes—all of them—with ease by agreeing to measure objectively the plausibility of the diverse opinions under dispute, and then to opt for the most plausible one, whatever it may turn out to be.

This suggestion is obviously futile, as no criterion exists for a measure of plausibility, let alone one generally endorsed. (Philosophers are aware of this fact, as they declare the measure of plausibility to be a probability measure and they admit that they have no idea how to apply it as they have no idea what that measure is. Their interest is to explain the agreement that prevails in science, not in practical affairs. They suggest that were we all more scientifically-minded there would be less dispute all round and so les strife. These philosophers are convinced that this is fine even though admittedly full of holes, since science is so successful. In truth, however, science is so successful because it engages its adherents in constant disputes with very clear-cut means for their resolution by appeal to experience.) Naturally, in any dispute, theoretical or practical, the different parties are disposed to consider different view the "most plausible" (which is the source of the dispute.) Skeptical considerations suggest at once that it is impossible to measure the plausibility of statements, let alone to do so objectively. (We present skepticism in some detail in the Appendix.)

One need not be a confirmed skeptic to doubt the viability of this idea: it is too good to be true. Indeed, it was first proposed by Laplace, the famous philosopher-mathematician-physicist, about two centuries ago. Were it true, its application would be so successful in amicable terminations of disputes that its employment would become very common. As we know, this is not exactly the case. Of course, advocates of this popular suggestion have good explanations for the failure of their method, but these are irrelevant here, as what matters here is their failure to overcome the glaring insufficiency of their method. The potential success of their method rests on the possible general acceptability of some criterion for the plausibility of opinions; and until such a criterion becomes broadly accepted, this method is still futile. Oddly, Laplace was well aware of the Utopian character of his proposal, as he expected it to prevent wars. He suggested that the very possibility of rational resolutions of all disputes, no matter how remote, should suffice to convince people to see that replacing fighting with rational means is advisable even without the ability to offer detailed rational means for the resolution of all disputes. We laud this; we think that it is indeed wise to replace war with rational means; the rational means, however, are those of tough negotiations and tougher debates. We hope to be able to show you how, and in sufficient detail for you to start practicing, not in the prevention of the next world war, but in things —theoretical or practical—that you judge significant and that are within your province.

Allow us to make a small digression so as to introduce some historical perspective, so as to update our mention of the utopian nature of the desire to avoid all dispute and all conflict that characterized the last thinker of the Age of Reason. A century later, the rise of modern logic re-raised the utopian hopes among disciples of the famous philosopher Ludwig Wittgenstein, among them Rudolf Carnap in particular, that they would convince every reasonable person in the absolute objectivity of their philosophy. This forced them to view most people around, particularly peers, as not quite reasonable and even as not quite honest. Ironically, they were not in agreement among themselves about politics (some but not all of them were socialists). Hence, they failed to agree about the use of their own criterion to resolve their own disagreements to their own satisfaction, let alone do so with their opponents, not to mention their inability to communicate on anything with the people who could (and alas! soon did) declare war. War was declared, and the most devastating ever, yet Carnap went on with his project, and in 1950 offered a book with a detailed presentation of the machine that Laplace had dreamt about. As it happened, this machine can say very little; it could not even say that $2+2=4$. Posterity finally pronounced him and his peers unreasonable and their philosophy lost its once tremendous popularity (due to the hope to alleviate the frustration that debates cause). Ultimately, then, the suggestions of the followers of Wittgenstein are as obviously inapplicable as they looked before he entered the scene. The suggestions we endorse here, by contrast, are applicable, and even with ease, but their promise is much less grandiose.

Let us then add a note on the psychological process involved here, since we are wary of calling irrational or blocked the people who do not share our views. On the contrary, we find it reasonable to assume that our views on disagreement are not shared by most people, ignorant and learned, plain and sophisticated. Attitudes to disputes are often quite ambivalent, for reasons that we have already sketched. Thus, engagement in disputes that most people in contemporary society participate in, are mixed with a sense of satisfaction that is often strongly tied in with a sense of dissatisfaction. It likewise often comes with a sense of strong bonding that is often strongly tied in with a sense of strife. Thus, even when the use of our recommendations increases efficiency and pleasure, it may also incur displeasure. In such cases, when the stress is becoming overwhelming and the debate is not utterly mandatory, the wise thing to do is to stop it: fighting ambivalence head-on is always unwise. Notoriously, alas, ambivalence often blocks this move too, as usually ambivalence is tied in with obsessive insistence (including the insistence on efforts to solve problems unaided and the refusal to consider help or advice). Therefore, in all cases in which our suggestions incur pain—in any way—we suggest that you desist from employing them.

In disagreement with all the philosophers tainted with the utopianism of Wittgenstein, we say this. Some disputes cannot be resolved. This does not make them less real; on the contrary; pain is always real, no matter how unreal or unnecessary its cause may be. Obviously we should not hope to attain the impossible. Nevertheless, continuing engagement in impossible pursuits may be great fun. As long as you find the very search enjoyable, you need not worry about Wittgenstein telling you to stop your search, of course, and you may increase the pleasure of the search if you will be patient, and you will be patient if you realize that some disputes are hard to resolve. They are usually theoretical, and theoretical research is known to be a cause of pleasure and of frustration. So it is better to be cautions. Our aim here is practical (even regarding theoretical affairs). And we remain cognizant of the fact that in the world of practice disputants are keen to resolve as many disputes as they can and as rapidly as they can.

We will go further. We do not know what is possible and what is impossible. Most of the things that we take for granted today were deemed impossible but one century ago, not to mention the sages of ancient times whose ideas still have enormous influence on us to this very day. Bernard Shaw said, "The reasonable man adapts himself to the world; the unreasonable one persists in trying to adapt the world to himself. Therefore, all progress depends on the unreasonable man." What he meant, of course, is that what some people consider unreasonable as a matter of course turn out to be eminently reasonable, and we owe this progress to people with vision who dare doubt common wisdom. The conclusion from this is, do not rush to dismiss the unconventional. They may be in error, as regrettably we all so often are; if you take them seriously, argue with them. They may show you in error, and you may show them in error. Assuming we are all sufficiently open-minded to learn, of course.

Plato said, theoretical disputes too must come to rest. He declared unserious those who taught differently, the leading sophists—the then experts in the art of disputation who made a living teaching it to budding politicians. He said that if we are after the truth (rather than after fame and fortune) as we should be, then we should strive to end each important dispute with the truth in hand. He charged the sophists with insincerity, ascribing to them relativism about the truth: the theory that *truth is not an absolute;* your truth is different from my truth. This appalled Plato, and his charge that the sophists were insincere is reasonable when applied to those sophists who were indeed relativists. All of them, including the postmodernists, assert that there is no one absolute truth, that all truth is relative. Hence, more than one party to a dispute is in possession of some sort of a truth, and hence that resolutions of disputes are neither necessary nor possible. Indeed, they declare as an absolute truth, debates are absolutely redundant. We reject wholeheartedly all forms of relativism, including postmodernism. We consider it a dangerous absurdity (the absurdity of the absolute rejection of the absolute truth). Admittedly, we do ignore many promises that we find impossible to fulfill, but if we like them, then we do so with heavy hearts. Relativists, including postmodernists, promise the impossible conquest of the need to argue. Let us repeat: people go on arguing despite the frustration that this activity incurs, since *its avoidance is even more frustrating than its persistence*. Some postmodernists admit this; they have two different ways to overcome this objection to their philosophy.

Their first way of overcoming this objection to relativism is by differentiating between terminable and interminable disagreements and admitting ways to overcome this objection to their philosophy that the terminable ones are open to debate but to insist that ways to overcome this objection to their philosophy are not the interminable ones. (Assuming that Wittgenstein was a relativist in his old age, then we may ascribe to him this move. Yet he then no longer claimed to know which debate is terminable, which not.) Moreover, this defense of relativism rests on the assumption that participants in debates can know that their debates are terminable. Terminable debates, some relativists say, take place within premises that are not open to debate. Thus, the terminable debate will be terminated differently when the parties to the debate are Christians than when they are Buddhists. Debates about the choice between these two religions are interminable, as each faith comes as a relative truth.

The second way to overcome the objection to relativism is to undergo a "detoxification program", to receive training to prepare us to learn to live happily without the need for debates and thus avoid the frustrations that they incur. Those making this proposal offer a choice: we may go into seclusion to follow some postmodernist program, or continue practicing debates despite frustration, or attempt some method (such as the one we offer in this handbook) that helps to reduce the frustration of your debates considerably while increasing its fruitfulness and taking you to new intellectual vistas.

Indeed, as noted above, the proposal to avoid dogmatism, that we take here as the default proposal, all thinkers endorse with the exception of some relativists. (Opponents of relativists rightly assert that they cannot avoid dogmatism; yet, as discussion about this assertion lies beyond the scope of this handbook, we will not insist on this here.) Our default proposal rests on the fact, as also noted above, that dogmatism frustrates: dogmatists may argue, and even avidly, yet by definition they will not budge. If all parties to a dispute are dogmatists, frustration is assured; moreover, it is assured to rise with the ongoing insistence to continue the (clearly futile) debate.

There can hardly be any objection to the proposal to avoid dogmatism; we do not make it, however, given that avoidance of dogmatism seems to us inoperable. Very few dogmatists admit openly that they are dogmatic. On the contrary, most dogmatists are profoundly convinced that their advantage over their opponents is that they have *overcome* all dogmatism and thus they can and do see the naked truth. The following (ancient and mediaeval) proposal was popular in the Age of Reason: whenever you are sure that you are right, seek some wise people who disagree with you and ask them to argue with you about your conviction. This advice is hardly any good, since those who fail to see the naked truth hardly count as wise. This is a catch. How then are we to overcome it?

During the Age of Reason, the popular view on the matter was psychological. It was Francis Bacon's idea that dogmatism is a kind of self-flattery. Traditional self-flattery is similar to today's ego-involvement: it is the received opinion (dogma?) that good will should suffice as a tool for overcoming all dogma and all prejudice. Bacon proposed that we should all contribute to the common good by doing some research, and that doing so requires good will in two ways, first in overcoming our disposition towards self-flattery and second in devoting time to research. This is lovely, but not quite true; many dogmatists are full of good will, yet they are unaware of their own dogmatism and ego involvement—perhaps with good reasons. Clearly, good will alone is insufficient as a cure for dogmatism. Moreover, how does one create the needed good will?

Thus, quite contrary to common wisdom, we regretfully admit that we *are all dogmatic to varying degrees*. To claim oneself free of all dogma, said the wise philosopher Bertrand Russell, is humbug. He did not take this as a sign of defeat. On the contrary, it is heartwarming that, the ubiquity of dogmatism notwithstanding, people do manage to change views and learn from experience, even if there still is much room for improvement. Indeed, how else is the little progress that we experience at all possible? Here common experience is the very opposite to common wisdom: however dogmatic we may be, we all are susceptible to facing strong arguments that force us to give up some dogmas, no matter how hard we may try to stick to them. Indeed, how else do people lose their faith in the ugliest aspects of the religions of their forefathers? They may deny this, yet no Catholic sides with the Inquisition these days, and no Lutheran will sanction Luther's proposal to burn synagogues, and no Jew advocates an eye for an eye. The ability to learn is more pronounced in cases of people's desertion of newfangled religion surrogates like Marxism, Freudianism, scientism, and other systems.

Our question, then, is the following: what is the most efficient, rational way to treat disputes? How should we steer clear of excessive dogmatizing and excessive toleration of error? How can we avoid despair and argue reasonably while treating the views we hold with a right measure of skepticism and while keeping our expectations not too high and not too low?

All this would be much easier to discuss were it possible to decide in advance how much time and effort the termination of any given dispute requires. We would then be able to decide whether the investment of time and effort in debate on a given question is worth our while or not. This, however, is in principle impossible. Evidently, then, we may err in our assessment of the time and effort required, and then our efforts to close a debate successfully may be futile and thus frustrating. This raises an additional question: when is it wise to continue *despite* frustration, and when is it wise to yield to it and stop the debate? This, again is the same as in any prospecting venture, or any venture at all. Thomas Alva Edison said, "Many of life's failures are people who did not realize how close they were to success when they gave up." Obviously, this is only half of the story: many of life's failures are people who did not realize how far they were from success when they refused to give up despite repeated frustration. Frustrated parties to disputes continue in desperate efforts to conclude them and thus overcome frustration. And indeed, no one wishes to quit when success is around the corner. Yet success may elude us, repeatedly seeming to be hiding just around the corner. When then should participants to a dispute curtail it? When does it cease to make sense to continue a debate? And if we stop the argument, under what conditions does it make sense to reopen it?

Debates About Theories

Before continuing with this vexing question, we should make another necessary detour in order to avoid some common pitfalls, in order to avoid frustrating you as a reader of this handbook. We sincerely wish you to enjoy reading it.

Our interest here is limited to cases of disputes about the truth. Is the opinion under dispute true? Which of the alternative answers to a given question is true? Not all arguments are devoted to the search for the truth. For example, people may tell lies and argue in effort to make their opponents believe their lies. For another example, people may argue about the price of a product in order to negotiate a compromise. Even in such cases, however, at least some disputes involve questions to which the true answer is unique. In the case of a debate about the right price of a given commodity, the relevant question to which there is a unique true answer is, what is the price of the product that is the lowest that seller is willing to accept, and what is the highest price that buyer is willing to pay? (Clearly, these two may differ, in which case there may be no deal: trade may be frustrating too.)

Our interest here is to help you develop debating skills, and so we will limit our presentation to cases of rational debates, or, more generally, we will concentrate on disputes whose participants try to behave within reason: we will discuss cases of disputes that are rationally conducted to include the rational decision to open a debate or not, and if so, on what conditions. (For a conspicuous example, if you can, do not open a debate under stress or when you are busy or distracted but postpone it to a more propitious moment. Of courses, this may become a technique of procrastination that is a mode of self-deception. Obviously, those engaged in undesired disputes, especially if they are people who wish to win at all costs, have to take stock and come to some general tough decisions.)

Here we go with the general trend of the literature on disputes, since it ignores self-deception (unless it is concerned with obsessive contrariness) as well as efforts to win by foul means (unless its concern is with magic tricks or with manipulative techniques like brainwashing). The one exception to this concerns rhetoric: the literature pays attention to the distinction between rational arguments and rhetoric, where the default aim of rational argument is the truth and that of rhetoric is to win one way or another, to convince. Since rhetoric follows different methods than rational debates, the literature should ignore it, yet since Plato and Aristotle paid much attention to it, tradition does the same. Tools specific to rhetoric—to efforts to convince by any means—are emotional, aggressive (raising one's voice) or amiable (conveying or inviting sympathy). They intrude rational debates but should stay marginal. Otherwise they become anti-rational; they are then deliberately manipulative and may even use inferences known to be invalid. Still, as marginal they have one role to play that is reasonable—as long as they remain marginal. It is this: in public debates, especially in politics, one who is ready for a rational debate may bump into a rhetorician who spoils the game. The question is, what does one do under such circumstances? In western movies the hero draws a gun and forces liars to show the cards that they have up their sleeve; in domestic comedies chess players stop the game when they face a breach of the rules of the game. In private debate, we have said repeatedly, the way to treat a frustrating debate—and this usually involves violations of the rules of debate—it is likewise advisable to stop the debate. But in public this luxury may be unavailable. Similarly, unavailable is the method of exposing the rhetorician as a rhetorician. There are however simple techniques that most of the time suffice for overcoming the unpleasant situation. We will state them now and then ignore rhetoric as much as possible.

First, let us observe: like prejudice, rhetoric is never fully avoidable. As it is unavoidable, the limit of its use is an unproblematic matter of commonsense. Hence, no argument is fully rational. Relativists use this as proof that there is no rational debate, only rhetoric. (No one is totally clean; hence, no one is dirty. Hence, let us wallow in dirt, or at least do not condemn me for my disposition to do so.) We wish to ignore both the rather non-rational and the distinctly anti-rational arguments here. They have their place, of course, but not in the present handbook, in which we aim to reduce frustration that debates incur and to increase of their fruitfulness. Indeed, rhetoric can only increase frustration. All too often, rhetoric succeeds in helping to close a debate, but the cost of this success is increased frustration as the losing party realizes that they yielded only because they were successfully manipulated. So let us close this point by mentioning the few simple rules that should suffice to encounter the excessive rhetoric that threaten to bring the rationality of a public debate to utter ruin.

The most important thing to remember is not to lose your cool. This is the prime target of able rhetoricians and you should not let them have the pleasure of seeing you lose our cool. Wait for your turn and be ready to respond to the rhetorician only when you are clearly expected to do so, and even then count to 10 before answering. Second, repeat the point or the line of argument of the rhetorician; make it as verbatim as you can and do not make it a caricature. This done, the damage that the rhetoric has caused is almost totally repaired. What is missing is a simple assessment of the rhetoric that the audience has just heard. After that you can count to 10 again and continue as if the incident has never happened. If all this does not work, you can shrug your shoulder—literally—and cut your losses.

A general note on Dialectics and Rhetoric. The word "dialogue" means two people talking; one proposes a theory and answers questions that the other asks in effort to criticize that theory. The dialectical method is the way a rational argument is conducted on a given question: competing answers to it are examined in search for the truth (or at least the approximation to the truth). This activity is the concern of this handbook. The difference between them has engaged thinkers through the ages, as it is the concern of a famous early dialogue of Plato (Gorgias). Nevertheless, efforts were repeatedly made to show these two to be the same. Traditionally, as Plato has put it, the aim of dialectic is to refute and of rhetoric to persuade. Since the rules of the two procedures are identical, it is understandable that people wish to identify them, especially those thinkers who deemed the real aim of refutation is to clear the way to persuasion. Nevertheless, obviously the use of the tools specific to rhetoric in efforts to criticize is very limited; the role they play in efforts to persuade is a matter of psychology that we will try hard to ignore.

To sum it up, dialectic and rhetoric should follow the same rules, yet the temptation to cheat or break the rules is great in rhetoric and small in dialectic. The aims of the players nevertheless influence conduct within these rules in subtle and uninteresting manners. Still, the most significant difference may relate to cheating: cheating defeats the purpose of dialectic, and so it is in the interest of the players to behave as honestly as they know how. In rhetoric, cheating that is not caught may be just what is required to make a difference between win and loss. A subtle difference is this: in a dialogue it always pays to admit errors and ignorance, and in rhetoric it is often better to conceal them. The rules of the game require that one answer truthfully when asked about these things, but if the opponent overlooks them, then a good rhetorician will let it ride. Another subtle difference is this: when the discussion approaches a doubtful area, the dialectician would wish to learn something about it and participate in the inquiry into that area; a good rhetorician might then make an effort to lead the debate in different directions. The rules require that consent of the opponent is necessary for such a move, of course, but a good rhetorician will tempt the opponent to move to an area that may deceptively look more promising.

As our concern here is to reduce frustration, we suggest that often frustration is the outcome of a debate that looks dialectical to one party and rhetoric to the other. We are not interested here in rhetoric, even though we do admit that at times it serves its users well. We are trying to help a dialectician, especially a beginner dialectician, and only by listing the situations that are frustrating, in order to help change or avoid them. How then should one who is seeking the truth and is engaged in a private debate handle the rhetoric that may sneak into the debate? We suggest that the answer is relatively simple. Assume that your opponents are dialecticians and not rhetoricians. Make sure that they do not violate the rules of the game. If you are not sure, say so, and, we suggest, stop the debate for a while and begin a (meta-) debate about the rules. If the opponent plays by the rule, wins, and is happy about it, just ignore this fact and ask yourself if you have benefitted from the debate. If not, be less eager to open a debate with the same party than before. Remember, the joy that an opponent derives from having won a debate is childish and it should not upset you. Remember, the joy derived from a good debate—and debate should be very joyful—is from having learned from it.

The study of rhetoric is vast. Many studies in the field of psychology are devoted to its character and influence; these issues, once again, lie beyond the scope of this handbook. To make sure that we discuss dialectic and not rhetoric even though there is no clear-cut division between them, we apply a distinction similar to the one used in linguistics between competence and performance. When linguists study the rules of proper speech, they take as their data for research the grammar that native speakers display, and then these linguists must ignore cases of clearly substandard performance—due to neglect or other factors, such as fatigue, limited memory span, or even plain ignorance. For, they are interested in rules displayed not in any performance but in the performance of the competent, namely in the conduct of native speakers able to follow the rules. They seek rules by the study of the conduct of following these rules. The task is subtle: linguists want to avoid idealizing and stay with grammar of a living language and avoid errors of earlier linguists; yet when they seek rules by studying proper speech they idealize. This cannot be helped, and the only tools at the hand of the linguist are commonsense and the critical attitude. We too are not interested in performance, such as trying to win, but rather in the competent use of rational argument only, and we too try not to idealize too much but are aware that some idealization is unavoidable. Therefore, if you learn to follow the traditional rules that we describe more or less, perhaps you should be content and not invest the excessive efforts that may frustrate. You can use rising frustration as a meter: when this happens try to do something about it, perhaps simply do something completely different for a while. Contrary to most handbooks, this one rests on the supposition that trying hard is often self-defeating.

Our interest in the rules then is not theoretical but practical: knowledge of these rules should render debates both less frustrating and more fruitful. (These two, we repeatedly claim, go together.) To take a practical example, lawyers in courts aim to win, but since the aim of the court is to find the truth (and to act upon it in accord with the law of the land), its conduct is following the rules of rational debate. This is not to say that all court procedures are as rational as they can be, since lawyers can and often do use rhetoric, but the task of the judge is to warn the jury not to be swayed by rhetoric and to curb the lawyers' rhetoric if it is excessive. At times judges take bribes, of course, but then in the study of the rules that courts should follow their conduct is ignored since bribery is obviously against the rules of every civilized court-procedure.

Thus, we had to begin with helping you to be able to neutralize rhetoric, as it is a major source of frustration in debates. We want to help you distinguish with ease—in debates that you may encounter—between cases of performances that display competence and those that do not, namely, between rational and non-rational aspects (we have already discussed the anti-rational aspects as best we could). Some non-rational tools are unavoidable, but fortunately they are such that once you are aware of the way in which they work, their influence diminishes or even disappears and you can overlook them with profit. The paradigm case is being aware of the fact that a raised voice intimidates; you know that you should neutralize its effect with little or no effort. If you find it hard to resist the intimidating effect of an argument, however, then we strongly recommend that you should stop the debate. At times stopping is not an option; under such conditions, the frustration is caused not by ignorance of the rules of debate but rather by violence. Discussion of violence disguised as rational argument (a. k. a. brainwashing) lies beyond our scope of this handbook. Needless to say, though, people in the unfortunate situation of suffering from harassment should know that they face an irrational situation that cannot be guided by the norms of rational debate. This does not neutralize the frustration, but it does eliminate an aspect of it that is very annoying, namely, not seeing how the bullies manipulate us. Seeing it enables us to seek improvement—of kinds that we cannot discuss here.

In other words, mere awareness comprises but a partial solution. Cases such as brainwashing in prisoners-of-war camps, in particular, are more challenging. They involve non-rational arguments, yet awareness of the situation does not void the influence of the arguments being employed. But even in these cases, those aware of the brainwashing attempt are usually much less influenced than those who are not.

Our rule here then is dual: avoid using rhetoric and ignore your opponent's use of it as much as you reasonably can, or else stop the debate if you can. Common wisdom suggests fighting rhetoric, such as, for example, demanding of our opponents that they lower their voices. We decidedly avoid making this suggestion, as it is futile and even counterproductive. (It can be useful in court, to repeat, but it is not the concern of this handbook.) Ignoring the volume of the speaker and ignoring the aggressive words in written correspondence is more useful than protest, but if shouts and aggressive words persist and distract the debate, we recommend that it cease. (Before that we recommend that in the reply you quote the passages that you respond to, but quote them not verbatim.) Cases in which the prevention of annoyance is impossible are cases of harassment. They have little to do with argument and have no room in this handbook.

And so back to the question, when should participants to a dispute curtail it? When does it cease to make sense to continue a debate between well-intending parties? Yet before discussing the rational termination of a debate, we should ask, when is it rational to begin it? For, obviously, the better the debate is prepared, the less likely are the parties to encounter the need to terminate it abruptly. (This is true of all human encounters, of course.) When, then, is it rational to begin a debate? What are the prerequisites for a rational debate?

We stress this point, since readiness to stop a debate with opponents who violate the rules may render debates successful as it is the best way to bring opponents back to following the rules. As an illustrative example, consider refereed fights in a ring that follow clear rules. Contrast them with street brawls that do not. Most debates in modern society take place in living rooms between friends and thus, quite counterintuitively, they resemble street brawls more than scientific or parliamentary or court debates. Hundreds of books about debates are now on sale. Most of them offer strategies for successful use in high-school debating societies or techniques regarding how-to-win-a-debate-without-losing-a-friend. This book differs from these guidebooks mainly in two ways. First, our aim is to guide you not to win a debate but rather to benefit from it with as little frustration as is reasonable. Second, these guidebooks concentrate on rhetoric, while we discuss the rational conduct of debates and let the better idea win. For example, guidebooks often include suggestions such as "refrain from saying *you* are wrong" or "smile when disagreeing." Do not expect this kind of suggestion in this book. We will discuss here the logic of debate, not its wrappings, especially not ones that we do not find particularly agreeable.

Chapter 3
Improving the Wording of the Questions Under Dispute

Abstract Make sure that the debating parties agree as to what is the question under dispute. The question should be worded as an interrogative sentence (one that begins with a question word and ends with a question mark). Questions with vague wording such as, "how about x, y or z?" are better not taken up. The same goes for unspecified questions, like the question of this or that topic or person or situation. Do not debate definitions of concepts. Instead of trying to argue about the "right" definition of a certain concept, clarify its meaning by presenting examples, mainly paradigm cases. (If the concept is technical, its definition is usually not under dispute.) Once the question under dispute and the presuppositions behind it are reasonably clearly stated and agreed upon, the debate can start. Notably, there is no need to worry whether this precondition has been sufficiently met or not: if the background information proves not to be adequately clear and the debate starts getting frustrating, then it is always possible to take a step back and discuss the background material a bit more before proceeding.

Here is a reasonable advice: do not rush into a confrontation. You are not obliged to respond to a challenge positively or negatively. Except for cases where the law imposes a confrontation, you may ignore it. The challenger may call you a coward and otherwise tease you; this is childish. Any response to a challenge has its costs and benefits, and it is wise to assess these before doing anything. Of course, there are exceptions. At times there is little or no time for deliberation. In such cases there is no room for advice. At times you may see the challenge coming and you may prepare your possible responses to possible sorts of challenge. These cases are so rare that we will be forgiven if we ignore them.

To repeat, some debates are obligatory. They may be legally or at least morally obligatory; or our bosses may impose them on us. The paradigm case is indeed the court case: it is usually dumped on us; we often have no choice but to participate in the action, to take sides, to argue our cases or opinions as best we can. Even then, it is not clear whether we are invited to apply the rules of dialectic or of rhetoric. All too often lawyers take it for granted that rhetoric is superior to dialectic. Indeed, they say that when dialectic is superior to rhetoric, then obviously rhetoric recommends dialectic, so that it always has priority. This is a sleight of hand. In courts we want judgment in our favor; in dialectic we want the better opinion to win. Is it right to aim to win a case in court at all cost? Some lawyers take it for granted that it is.

And then these lawyers take it for granted that they have no moral obligation as long as they avoid penalty for contempt of court. We think that even pragmatic reasons render this kind of conduct undesirable. But as this is no handbook on lifestyles, we let this ride.

One way or another, for most people in contemporary society most debates are optional. (Lawyers, physicians and researchers are the exception, and they are the minority.) In many circles, it is customary to challenge people to argue, and it is considered dishonorable to dodge the challenge. Yet it is usually unwise to jump right in without forethought; the right to decide which conflicts to enter and which to avoid is valuable. We assume that in some cases, people can exercise their right to choose which debate to instigate or to join. And then, to repeat, each decision incurs its costs and its benefits. We should mention here that one who belongs to a circle in which challenges to argue are too frequent or too rare may consider the option of moving from their circle to more normal ones and figure their cost-benefit accordingly.

We should then specify here the difference between practical (obligatory) and theoretical (non-obligatory) debates. The usual distinction between practical and theoretical debates rests on the suggestion that there is no use for theoretical debates, or at least no need for them. Both these suggestions are greatly mistaken. Also, their refutations are obvious. One of them is the fact that practically all of today's technology is science-based and that research in science is chiefly theoretical. Criticism is the heart and soul of rational debate, and with no criticism there is no theoretical progress. Moreover, learning is a basic need (albeit, as Abraham Maslow has notes, less basic than the needs for food and for company). Still, although we feel a strong need to learn as much as debate provides a learning tool, we always have a choice when it comes to any specific item that we may wish to learn. Here there is the question of opportunity cost: we all want to know more things than we can learn. Hence, if we invest in learning one item we thereby give up learning another. Assuming that we have a limited budget that we utilize as best we can (in this case it is the time to allot to learning), the cost of the acquisition of each item (in this case, of knowledge) is the giving up of other options that it ousts. This is known as opportunity cost. Members of different circles, to repeat, may allot different spans of time for debate. In each, however, there is opportunity cost for debating time. The wise does not squander it.

Once you decide to enter a debate, the first prerequisite for an enjoyable and hopefully fruitful debate is to frame a good question. This is easier said than done. What question is good, then? This is one of the toughest questions in the diverse set of situations that call for debate, including every field of learning. For, even those interested in a specific field or sub-field of learning must find a specific question within it that they find particularly interesting and that they consider promising to investigate. We know that some past studies in these fields were very fruitful and we usually ascribe it to their success in part to the wise choice of a problem. In specific cases we even go further and say, the choice of a question was itself a great contribution to human knowledge, as it was a replacement for some traditional questions that had gone stale and so it was a great improvement on it. For example, modern science emerged (as a scientific revolution) in the seventeenth century when (among other things) researchers stopped asking what is the essence of things, or what are the teleological reasons underlying their presence, and started asking what things are made of and how they move around. Moreover, a great change in the scientific revolution was a shift (that Johannes Kepler effected) from the question, how can orbits of planets be described with least deviations from the ideal circular orbits, to the question, can the orbits be not circles?

If a particular question interests you sufficiently and you share it with anyone in the vicinity—be it in a quest to contribute to human knowledge or only to please your own self—you can suggest to open a debate on it. This condition, however, may be too constraining (as it is hard to find a shared interest) and not suffice to create fruitful dialog (since the interesting question can be too difficult and none of you can come up with any answer to it). For example, theological questions bore many people, yet they interest many; yet debates on them are stale and very frustrating. Such things are of course alterable. Consider the questions, why the sky is blue, or why is the grass green; these always interested many researchers but until a little over one century, no one came up with a possible answer to them. It turns out that the blueness of the sky is much easier to explain than the greenness of grass. This no one could imagine before the answers were given.

One rule of thumb for the avoidance of frustration (whenever it is applicable) is to choose a good controversial question. A question is controversial if competing answers appear in the literature (including the internet). It is a good question if the parties to the dispute agree that the answers of their competitors are reasonable. This is obviously not always possible: the question on the agenda may be new, for example, or it may have been absolutely overlooked to date, or there were no answers to them for debates about them to proceed. But whenever this option is applicable, it saves the frustration of futile debate.

We consider this a matter of great importance: arguments against worthless opinions tend to be intellectually worthless. Of course, they may be valuable otherwise. In particular, there may be a great social need to argue against worthless opinions simply because they are widespread and harmful. The paradigm case is racism. Criticizing racism is important as educational act, but usually it makes no intellectual sense to debate with a racist. As it happens this obvious fact has a strong scientific basis. It is this. Racists used traditionally intuitive ideas about race that did not make much scientific sense. The modern racists claimed to be applying Darwinian ideas. They argued that the human race needs protection by eliminating undesirable genes from the common gene pool. This claim is erroneous: Darwinism relies on natural selection and so it does not call for intervention. The racists answered this by claiming that the contemporary humane treatment of degenerate samples that should be eliminated by natural selection block this selection and threatens humanity. This answer is contrary to the Darwinian idea that a wide gene pool is superior to the filtered one that prefers blue-eyed blond-haired fair-skinned individuals and excludes others. It is amazing that such great biologists as Conrad Lorenz, later a Nobel laureate, supported the Nazi racial segregation during World War II in a scientific paper. Yet today anyone who cares to study the matter learns fast that racism is an idea too easy to criticize. This, however, does not close the social need to criticize it publicly. A good question to debate, though, is, what is the best way to overcome racism—or xenophobia in general.

A pointless debate, even when necessary, is tedious and frustrating and quite unenlightening for the better informed. Unfortunately, this handbook offers little advice to alleviate educational frustration. We suggest that our readers consider debates that they have some information about, and ask themselves whether *the debated issue is useful and whether the debate is held between respectful parties*. Obviously, racists are no respectful party. We suggest that you debate only under the two conditions of respect for your opponents and usefulness of debates with them. Arguing with the young and with other kinds of inexperienced people as a part of educating them may be enjoyable if we respect them and remember that they are at an unfair disadvantage. Otherwise, debate with a disadvantaged opponent will be very tedious and cumbersome as well as futile. Indeed, the identity and learning potentials of opponents plays a significant role in determining the utility of debates with them.

To summarize this point, in cases of debates voluntarily undertaken, our rule of thumb should be to choose a good question that you find interesting, important or urgent. A question should be considered good only if among the competing answers to it, at least one, but by far better two or more, seem to you reasonable. You can then consult the literature or friends (and better both), especially friends who share your judgment about what answers seem reasonable (or else you can debate this matter with them) but you do not agree about their truth or falsity, or at least about the question, which of the extant answers is the best. The purpose of limiting discussion to good answers is that it is all too easy and hardly reasonable to criticize answers that no reasonable people will defend (even such theoretical exercises may be needed for the purpose of improving the educational level of the electorate in a democratic society).

Of course, a good question may have unreasonable answers; this, indeed, is the usual case. We suggest, then, that you list all the answers you can think of, but discuss only the reasonable ones (according to your choice, preferably after discussion with others, and always keeping an open mind about the matter; otherwise you will be the dogmatists who know that others disagree with them but who dismiss them with finality). Of course, this is not always possible. The known answers to an urgent question may be all unreasonable. They are often even popular. In such cases, often those who hold the unreasonable answers not only deem them reasonable, but also deem unreasonable the known alternatives as well as the search for new ones. Obviously, these are the cases of dogmatists. In such cases, the very possibility of rational debates is questionable. If you overlook this fact, be prepared for frustration. And there are incentives for this. People who hold popular but unreasonable answers often wish to argue with their opponents, but they usually have no idea about the rules of rational debates and they aim at convincing their opponents, not at learning from them through debates. Whatever the challenge they present, arguing with them will only frustrate. We definitely recommend avoiding such debates or at least entering them with open eyes. If you must argue regarding unreasonable

3   Improving the Wording of the Questions Under Dispute   31

populist views, the following rules for preparation may hopefully yield fruitful debate.

Even if an interesting controversial question is agreed upon, there is no guarantee that participants in it will manage to sidestep frustration. Regrettably, many disputes frustrate as they are conducted in too confused a manner to be interesting or fruitful. Even when participants know the difference between clarity and confusion and prefer the one to the other, they may stay confused anyway. Much of the confusion that fairly educated people perpetrate dwells on the border between competence and performance that we have already visited; participants in them could improve their competence by paying some attention to the rules. To avoid at least some of this confusion, we suggest starting a debate, especially if you must argue with people whose views you do not consider very reasonable, by discussing some preliminary questions. If your opponent has no patience for them, it is most likely a situation in which rational debate is not possible in any case, and so it is better to give up hope of a fruitful discussion. If your opponent does have the patience, you may start with the following three questions:

1. What is the question put for debate?
2. Is the question interesting or important?
3. Can the answers under dispute be simultaneously true?

Consider the first question: what is the question? It is a somewhat surprising empirical fact that many people who regularly engage in debates (politicians, scholars, celebrities) are convinced that they know what question is under debate, and that all parties to the debate know it too and agree about it. Often, they only seem to know what the question is but they do not, as a simple test for knowing the question should illustrate. Yet the test is no good. For one thing, they suggest that they know the question when in response to the test they say its name or title. Obviously, confusion emerges when different questions have the same name. (One question having different names is less confusing than few questions have the same name.) At times, an old name of a question persists while the question has already altered or split. And so, to offer the name of a question is often fairly useless. At times, a question splits into a few sub-questions, and so we have to ascertain that all parties stick to the one sub-question that they agreed to discuss. In other instances, still, a question is specified by a descriptive phrase, such as "the race problem" or "the main problem in contemporary physics." This is too vague to prevent frustrations. Indeed, a good debate question requires an explicit statement. That is to say, it should open with an interrogative word (who, what, which, when, why, where) and end with a question mark.

If you take our advice and stop a debate with the question, what is the question under debate, you may be surprised at the hostility that you may generate. You will find that often people will try to overrule your question as distracting. This violates a very important rule of debate: your question (what is the question under debate here and now?) is technically known as a point of order, and points of order always have priority. (This is also open to abuse. The notorious Senator Joseph McCarthy repeatedly interrupted debates by declaring the wish to make points of order and then made speeches instead.) People may then object that discussing your question is both tedious and unnecessary, since the debate will make the answer to your question clear. This is an excellent point: it is always right to ignore difficulties that resolve themselves; alas, it happens to be amply refuted: clarity and vigilance about it are essential and they do not resolve themselves.

And so, the explicit wording of the question under debate as a question is very important and spending time about it is wise. And, as mentioned above, it is better to seek a verbal formulation in the form of a question proper than formulating it by reference to a concept or to an idiom, since concepts and idioms might refer to several different questions. By wording the question under debate, the parties to it can avoid wasting efforts in an apparent, seeming dispute. Whenever we find that we are engaged in a seeming dispute, it is wise to seek the real question that hides behind faulty wordings. For example, "the problem of poverty" may refer to several different questions. What is the moral responsibility of well-to-do people towards the poor? What is the most efficient way to reduce poverty? Whose duty is it to reduce poverty, the state or the community, or some other body? These and many other questions may meet the description "the problem of poverty". So, instead of debating on "the problem of poverty," we recommend that you start by formulating the specific question you are debating.

Moreover, some sentences are grammatically formulated as questions, but are not questions under dispute, and therefore should be avoided. Examples:

1. Does A relate to B? The answer is always "yes" (this is a point of logic).
2. What are the relations between A and B? (There can be infinitely many relations, most of them uninteresting.)
3. What is known about A? (There can be infinitely many true assertions that refer to any subject.)

Consider the first question (Does A relate to B?) for which, by logic, the true answer is always Yes. Proof: Assume that there is no relation between A and B. It follows that their names share the previous sentence. Hence they are related. Hence they are necessarily related. Indeed, this way it is provable that there are infinitely many relations between A and B, no matter what they are, which is the true answer to the second question. For example, one relation is that neither was mentioned in the first chapter of this book. This relation is clearly uninteresting, but it still is a relation. A similar consideration leads to the answer to third question.

Now, the above questions were taken here literally. This is often a mistake. Their vagueness is intended, and its aim is to provide latitude. Indeed, there is as much room for vagueness as the parties to the encounter feel comfortable with. They should know that to be fruitful a debate should start after vagueness is eliminated to a reasonable extent, on the understanding that the option is always open to return to the question and word it better still. If there is no agreement on this point, it is better for discussants to recognize the sad fact that at that stage they are not prepared for a debate, that to start it anyway will cause too much frustration. Admittedly, there is no guarantee against frustration, but there are fairly good guarantees for frustration, and debating vague questions is one of them. And so it is a fairly good guideline to suggest not to rush into a debate but to avoid frustration, say by efforts to avoid debates about vague questions as vagueness will almost guarantee that a debate will frustrate.

When considering the question on the agenda for debate, the contesting sides should also check the presuppositions to it. If the parties disagree about these presuppositions, then the question is not yet suitable as the subject of the dispute before this matter is cleared to the satisfaction of all parties to the debate. For example, when the question is "What is the explanation for (the occurrence of) A?" the presupposition is that A has occurred. If it did not, obviously there is often no point debating this question. When disagreement emerges regarding presuppositions, it may be useful to devote some efforts to a preliminary dispute. In court cases, for example, preliminary disputes are common; indeed, deliberations on a case may be put on hold for the preliminary dispute to be settled first. Moreover, during the Middle Ages, several disputes dealt with question of which is the "right" religion: Christianity, Islam or Judaism. These disputes presupposed that one of these religions is the right one, ignoring the (logical) option that none of them is. Nowadays, for instance, a popular debate involves the most efficient legislation to fight drug abuse. The presupposition behind these debates is that the government should fight drug-abuse. We will not delve here into the issue of whether or not the presuppositions to any given debate are true or false. Rather, we point out that the parties to a dispute should try to be aware of its presuppositions, and if one of them disagrees with the presupposition of a debate, then perhaps they would do better to abstain from it and suggest instead another, preliminary debate, concerning its presuppositions. One may, of course, join a debate on a presupposition that one considers false. This is known as supposition for the sake of the argument. Often such debates are theoretically instructive, say, if we are not dogmatic about our view that the presupposition is false, but also if we insist on it and rightly so. For, we may learn from this the extent of the damage that some false presuppositions cause.

So much for now on our first question, *what question is on the agenda for a debate*? Let us turn to the second question, then: is that question interesting? Alternatively, is it important? A question is not interesting and not important if the parties engaged in it do not mind what the right answer to it is. A question is certainly interesting or important in at least the following two kinds of cases:

1. The true answer to it has practical implications (for example, the question is medical and pertains to an urgent case).
2. If it is helpful in the discussion of an answer to one of the "big" or central questions that engage us constantly, such as, what is the meaning of life? (There is no point in asking whether this question is interesting, since no "bigger" questions exist; everybody can take interest in one or another component of this question).

Unfortunately, many well-known discussions refer to uninteresting questions. Consider the frequently asked kind of question, do males and females differ in regard to mathematical ability? Such a question is not interesting since, *a priori*, its true answer is obviously in the affirmative. The probability approaches zero that any observed ability of females and males is on the average exactly the same. Also, a demographic change may change the observed averages, but scarcely equate them. Statistically speaking, if the samples are large enough, you will almost always find a statistically significant difference between two independent sub-samples. The gender difference in any regard is only interesting (if at all) if it is big enough to be important. But then, one must decide in advance what the threshold for an interesting difference is. Moreover, since we all agree that mathematical ability depends to some extent on education, and since it is well known that girls in many societies are more discouraged than boys from studying mathematics, it is reasonable to expect females to show lower proficiency in mathematics. The useful question then is slightly different. It is, will their ability be still lower if they acquire equal education? Moreover, clearly, the question is affected by gender stereotyping: the stereotypical woman is better at doing work that the stereotypical man hates to do, and such men justify their expectation from women by holding low views of them, and they justify these low views of women by the claim that women are not good at math (regardless of most men being no good at math either). Since degrading stereotypes are better ignored without much ado, we recommend replacing the question about the relative proficiency of the genders in math with such questions as, what is the most efficient way to eradicate contempt in our society.

As another example consider the frequently asked questions: Who are the best X (for instance, who is the best singer or football player, or: Who was a better soccer player – Diego Maradona or Pele?). These questions are neither interesting nor important since they can hardly teach us anything about the big questions. One may sincerely claim that Pele was better player than Maradona, and another one may claim the opposite (and a third one may claim that they were at the same level). No matter who is right, none of the possible answers implies anything we know to the questions such as, what is the meaning of life, and none of them has any practical implication. It is amazing how frequently questions of this type of are under public discussion. Looking up websites such as Quora.com one may find many questions that have the following structure: What are some of the best …" These questions are not recommended for debate since they are not interesting. Anyone who could make them interesting will thereby make them candidates for interesting discussion and will thereby enrich our outlook.

Another kind of question that engages intellectuals and in many cases is guaranteed to frustrate is this: is an ability under discussion (say, the ability to learn a language) due to heredity or environment? Evidently, the answer is that both heredity and the environment contribute to every ability. Take language; as humans have the ability that other animals do not, heredity contributes to it; and as the ability expresses itself differently in different environments, say, children acquire their mother tongues, the environment contributes to it as well. Yet learned discussions of this question and of similar ones fill highly frustrating literatures.

So much for now on our second question, *is the question under debate interesting? Alternatively, is it important?* The third question that we recommend be examined before launching a debate is this. Can the answers under debate be simultaneously true? This question eradicates reasonably well (although not fully, of course) cross-purpose debates. For, if two answers are not mutually exclusive, then they are identical in content, or they are parts of one answer to a question, or else they do not answer the same question. Hence, if the answers to the given question can be simultaneously true, then either the dispute is not real or else it is too vague. The common confusion in such cases does not necessarily relate to one answer being given different wordings. To avoid this type of confusion is easy, by requiring that the answers be worded as similarly as possible, and that they include the question. Consider, for example a question of the kind, on what day of the week did a certain event happen? The answer "Sunday" should be replaced by, "the event happened on Sunday," and then all the answers—there are seven of them—should be worded the same way: "the event happened on ..." However, note that if the list of answers is complete, then all but one of the answers offered are false. If the disputing parties offer an incomplete list of answers, then all of them might be false. Regrettably, all too often, refuting all the available competing answers but one, is taken to be a proof of the non-refuted answer. This amounts to the supposition that the list of available answers is complete. All too often it is not.

Frequently the confusion lies elsewhere: the alleged answers are parts of one answer. We have a finite list of answers, and if the question invites a list of items (who belong to ...?), then each answer is a list. To be clear the controversial question should specify that it is answerable only by complete lists. And then, but only then, finding that a list is incomplete is a refutation of the answer. Otherwise, a partial list is an answers, and then a long list and a short one that it includes are two answers that will not be in conflict with each other. For example, the question, on which day of the week an establishment is open, if it is understood as a request for a complete list, then the list that mentions only two days will conflict with one that mentions three. Not otherwise. This is a vagueness that is better settled before the debate begins. Another vague well-known example of this kind depends on precise meaning of the word "better." Is the better good or not? (For example, although my better friends are among my good friends, a small obstacle being better than a big obstacle does not make any obstacle good.) Such words are *relative*, and so if the question under dispute concerns usage of such words, their exact meaning in the context of the dispute is better determined before it begins.

This kind of confusion can appear in somewhat more complex a situation. If each party to a dispute lists the benefits or the drawbacks of a certain item, then all positions can be simultaneously true, in which case (obviously) no genuine dispute exists. Especially since all those who defend monogamy, to take the paradigm that Bernard Shaw discussed (in his preface to *Getting Married*), name its merits and those who oppose it name its defects, the result is assured to be confusing. The debate can only start after each party offers two lists covering the benefits and the defects of monogamy, and if these lists are deemed complete then any discrepancy between them comprises a genuine dispute—but not necessarily otherwise; even if the lists are complete and identical, there can be a dispute if one party views the balance between these factors (the overall picture) differently from the other.

Admittedly, behind any case of a confused seeming-dispute, a genuine dispute may be lurking. And then it behooves the parties to the dispute to pull their resources together in order to word their dispute as best as they can before they continue with the arguments for and against this or that answer. Unfortunately, as Bernard Shaw has noted, quite frequently most bachelors argue by listing the advantages of bachelorhood and disadvantages of married life, whereas most married people argue the other way around. This makes no sense, as all sane people agree that both alternatives—any set of alternatives—under dispute is a mixed bag. Shaw, once again, found the debate more interesting if people exchange positions, so that bachelors argue against bachelorhood and *vice versa*. This suggestion is very wise, but not a part of the rules of debate (we will return to this later). The rule—try to avoid talking at cross-purposes—suggests that participants list the advantages and disadvantages of their alternative choices and debate them first if need be. Afterwards, when they reach sufficient agreement about the list of advantages and disadvantages of both each option, they can argue intelligently, interestingly and usefully about the question of which option is the better one. The preliminary discussion of the advantages and the disadvantages of the diverse options will prevent the frustrating situation of considering a minority opinion obviously true.

As it happens most political debates are frustrating because of the custom of listing only the benefits or only the defects of a given option. A possible excuse for this folly is that it is popular because it is properly applied in courts. Now even in courts wise lawyers concede to their opponents. (My client is no model citizen, but this is not at issue now, but rather the allegation that he has committed a crime that I will refute.) Moreover, in courts judge and jury take care of considering different parties. Thus, whereas under ordinary circumstances we may object to the question, did you stop beating your wife? since it is misleading, in court this question is not objectionable, since there are competing cross-examiners and the other one may rectify the impression by asking, why did you not stop? and provide the party under cross-examination the opportunity to say, because I have never started. Since political debates are not conducted as court procedures, each party must concede to the other or else misunderstanding is bound to occur. Of course, misunderstanding is never fully overcome, but all parties aiming at a balanced picture does help. This can be easily seen by comparing political debates in countries whose electorate are educated to varying degrees.

As it happens, there is one clear and easy means for overcoming the very frustrating situation of a minority opinion that seems obviously true and that is presented by opponents unfairly. It is one not likely to be taken at once in political debates, not even in countries with the best educated electorates. But it is easy to insist on it in scientific debates or between friends eager to learn. It is healthy then to ask intelligent opponents not to debate the opinion in question but rather to check that both parties agree on which question they disagree about. The first step to take is to check that the dispute is between parties that offer competing generalizations. When both parties to a dispute presents existential propositions (a sentence that starts with "there is" or a similar expression), then they have not presented a genuine dispute, although the situation indicates one—to be found in cooperative effort. If one party presents a general proposition and the other party presents an existential proposition, then either the other party disagrees with the one party without offering an alternative—which is quite legitimate, of course—or there is no dispute at all. These are cases where the agreement about the disagreement is easy to reach, although this is not always the case: disputes about definitions are persistently troublesome.

The matter of definitions is complicated, since statements that include descriptive terms like "the mill on the floss" are existential, yet the Mill on the Floss that George Eliot described is fictitious: it does not exist. This matter has troubled philosophers greatly. Fortunately, however, this issue pertains mainly to debates about logic, since in all other debates that refer to problematic matters, the parties can cut things short by agreeing as to what exactly they have in mind in the context of the debate. When explaining what the trouble is, things get usually sufficiently clear for those who wish to overcome the trouble in question, and it is advisable then to ignore matters of definition altogether. To take the funny example that philosophers waste ink on, when she wants to marry the mayor, perhaps she is in love with the fellow who happens to be the mayor and she may simply want to secure a good family life and so she goes for the mayor because he is available. Which option is true? This is a silly question, since when we care enough about the matter to discuss it, we can ask which option is true or conduct the discussion, whatever it is, once on the supposition that the one option is true and then that the other is.

The confusion regarding universals and particulars is prevalent in the arts, especially in philosophy. Words like "people" can serve either as a universal categorization ("all people") or as a particular one ("some people"). Many statements of the form "people are …" may be read as universal, and then as obviously false, or as particular, and then as obviously true. "People are sinners" is an example. Readers who stumble upon this statement face a dilemma: reading it as universal (all people are sinners) makes it trivially false, and reading it as particular (some people are sinners) makes it trivially true. The escape from the dilemma is to (mis) read this sentence to mean, "There is not a righteous man on earth who does what is right and never sins" (*Ecclesiastes*, 7:20). This is equivalent to the statement "All people commit some sins." This is not what the sentence in question says, and confusing the two sentences, the vague or ambiguous one and the clear one, is common in literature and literary debates. The incentive for it is to avoid explicit, blunt criticism of the vagueness of the vague proposition, on the false assumption that explicit blunt criticism is rude. We strongly suggest to avoid arguing with people who prefer not to state their criticism bluntly. If you must argue with them, all you can do is express regret for your need to offer your criticism explicitly and bluntly. This is quite advisable, since overruling people's sensitivity is regrettable indeed. Moreover, if you can, ask the people who make the vague statements to clarify them. If they do not and if you must continue with the debate regardless, then clarify the statement yourself, or offer competing clarification, as we have just done. This may get you out of a tough spot. But, to repeat our previously made point, there is never a guarantee for this and the present handbook is no devised for solving such problems; it can only touch upon the aspects of such problems that belong to the theory of argumentation.

Remember, then: some people are intent on proving themselves always right. When they say some vague or ambiguous sentence of this or that kind, they express indignation at people who read it as obviously false or as obviously true. We should ignore such responses, since it is never wise to argue with people who must always be right if it can be avoided: the only way to make sure that one does not say any false sentence in such a context is to keep silent. Some people prefer to talk not to the point. Our advice is to try to dissuade them, but not to make any effort if they refuse; it is easier to consider intended irrelevant talk a form of silence: you need not respond to it. On the whole, it is important to realize that you do not have to respond to anything said to you, except in courts, where you can appeal to the judge for help in case the layer who interrogates you does not behave by the book.

Many disputes, mainly in philosophy and in jurisprudence, concentrate on the clarification of the meanings of concepts involved in a given discussion. At times clarifications is obviously required. The paradigm case for this is when a speaker uses technical terms that are not familiar to their interlocutors. This is particularly important when the technical terms in question sound like ones that belong to ordinary parlance. Many philosophical disputes concern efforts to clarify ordinary well-understood concepts. Such clarifications may be helpful when the discussion refers to obviously vague or ambiguous terms that the parties can easily disambiguated, on the condition that the clarifications are not so detailed and lengthy that they will take up all the time allotted to the debate, leaving no time for the meat of the debate. This prolongation is assured by the demand for an ultimate definition for each and every concept involved. This is obviously impossible, since the search for them leads to an infinite regress: efforts to define the meaning of a concept involve more concepts, and they may want definitions too. Nor are definitions always the best means for clarification; paradigm cases are better for explicating the meaning of concepts. In most cases involving only normal parlance, clear examples are better than definitions. For example, instead of trying to define the concept "love" (which usually leads nowhere), it is better to give some examples of paradigm manifestations of love, especially in disputes that allot great importance to the difference between physical love (*eros*) and spiritual love (*agápē*). Finally, if two parties disagree about the meaning of a specific concept and the situation is otherwise relatively clear, then there is no need to resolve the difference: we can speak of that concept as Tom understands it, and of the same concept as Dick understands it, and so on. As long as we are careful enough to not confuse the meanings of Tom and of Dick, we are on safe ground. All we must remember here is that there is no such thing as "true meaning," only received meanings and other meanings clearly differentiated. If different disputants insist on different definitions, then this need not cause a dispute, as they can take care not to confuse the two meanings of the word and then the case is not different from any other case of one word with two meanings.

This is not to deny that even obvious words may invite clarification, say in cases of contested wills. This is a famously tough matter and courts are usually right when they try to avoid such discussions by suggesting compromises. We need not go into this matter here, as we have already explained. Let us take the opportunity, though, and note the obvious and oft forgotten difference between conflicting or contradicting opinions and conflicting interests. Conflicting or contradicting opinions cannot be simultaneously true; yet the assertion of conflicting interests is often true: it is true that both toddlers want to play alone with the same toy, even if this is impossible, yet the assertions that the toy belongs exclusively to one is in conflict or contradiction with the assertion that it belongs exclusively to the other. While this statement may seem too obvious, possibly it is not: followers of the famous philosopher Georg Wilhelm Friedrich Hegel, including all followers of Karl Marx, repeatedly confuse conflict with contradiction and they even use these two words as synonyms when they declare that some contradictions are true. This makes debate with them useless, since the way to help people see a mistaken of theirs is to show them that they contradict themselves. This obviously does not work if they respond with, "so much the better, showing me that this is inconsistent only reinforces my conviction that it is true." To argue with people who think so is obviously useless. The case is similar to that of a chess-player who is glad to sacrifice the king and is intent to go on playing after checkmate. More generally, it is better never to forget that we cannot force people to correct their mistakes. They can always stick to their errors by declaring your counter-example the exception that prove the rule, or that it is true in theory but not in practice, or by some other witticism or paradox.

Before we close this chapter, let us make one more suggestion that might reduce frustration in debates. Many people refer to debates as competitions of sorts, ones that we want to win. Losing a debate usually leads to frustration, like the disappointment we have when losing a competition. This need not be so. As long as you debate for the sake of research and of learning, you should consider it a success if you have learnt something interesting through it. Whether you win or lose should not matter. Nevertheless, many people do want to win, and get disappointed and frustrated if they do not. This is a psychological phenomenon, but it has its natural limitations. Thus, suppose you think that you have cancer and discuss the matter with your physician, who disagrees. Surely, you will be delighted to lose that debate. Consider error, at least a significant error, as a cancer of sorts, and you will see why Socrates insisted that defeat in a debate is the real win. Even in sports, whether physical or mental, when you are disappointed that you are less good a player than your opponent, you may enjoy the game and you may enjoy learning to improve. There is little more that we can say on this matter here.

A way that may reduce the influence of the sense of loss that accompanies defeat—in a debate or in any other game— is to make the best of it, as we have just noted. Another way is to remain aware of the desire to win throughout the game. As many psychologists have discovered, the very awareness of any irrational disposition decreases its intensity. Thus, for example, the awareness that a certain person irritated you for no good reason suffices to lessen that irritation somewhat. Finally, the most useful suggestion, already mentioned above: switch roles with your opponents. Try to argue for their position and against yours. This will lessen your sense of identifying with one side of the debate; consequently, you will care less about which side wins and more about the benefit accrued from the debate. You will identify more with your proficiency in the art of debate and enjoy the growth of self-esteem independently of what opinion you happen to consider the true answer to the question at hand.

In closing, let us expand a bit on the last suggestion. Usually, we do not expect people to present different sides of a dispute. For example, to repeat, the standard system that operates in courts worldwide expects each side to present one case, with no expectation of objectivity. The judge and the jury are expected to be objective and should therefore be a third independent party. We may consider unjust any violation of this method. For example, when a journalist interviews someone and functions as both prosecutor and judge and jury, we may say that the interview is not fair. The same may hold for business people in encounters with tax collectors. However, we suggest here quite a different view. When the aim of a debate is learning, the parties to it may benefit by switching positions; judge and jury are then redundant. This may also contribute to the efficiency of debates on practical matters, such as damage claims. If the plaintiff and defender change positions, even merely as an experiment, they may raise the possibility of reaching a reasonable compromise.

Chapter 4
The Burden of Proof

Abstract Pay attention as to who bears the burden of proof. Those who claim that their opponents are inconsistent should prove their claim (it is impossible to prove that one is consistent), and those who claim that a certain generalization is false should point at cases that refute it (there is no way to prove a factual generalization). Finally, the side that presents an existential statement (X exists) bears the burden of proof.

Once agreement about the question under dispute is reached, how is it possible to resolve rationally the dispute over the answers to it? What are the rational procedures for arguing or "proving" that your side is right and my side is not? Who should bear the burden of proof?

When someone presents an idea, one may meet one or the other of the following popular objections:

1. What you say is inconsistent (or inconsistent with a background idea that we share).
2. What you say is not new (someone else has already said it before).
3. What you say is trivial.

Suppose that you claim that your opponent's idea is inconsistent (or inconsistent with a background idea that we share). You then bear the burden of proof. Let us spell this out. You have to present the two statements that cannot be true together, show that they cannot be true together, and show that they follow from the idea that your opponent has expounded (with or without the background idea that we share, as the case may be). The individual who expounds the idea in question then has to accept your criticism, and then it is the end of the dispute until a corrected version of it is put for a renewed scrutiny. Alternatively, the burden of proof shifts to your opponent, whose task it is now to refute your criticism (namely, to point at a fallacy in your argument). Note that the presenter of the idea under scrutiny cannot prove that it is consistent. (Even the consistency of arithmetic is too much of a challenge: before the year 1900 or thereabout even the greatest mathematicians had no idea about how to begin to prove consistency.)

Consider the strangely popular debate on whether men or women are significantly oftener engaged in sexual intercourse. (The question can split to different questions about different kinds of sex: before or after marriage, with their spouse or out of marriage, etc.) Since the number of men and of women are approximately equal, and since usually every sexual intercourse involves a man and a woman, obviously both statements are inconsistent. (If we include homosexual intercourses, then the proof has to include the additional observation that homosexuality is equally common among men and women, so that homosexual intercourse is on the average equally common among the two genders.)

Such inconsistencies are rare. In many cases the consistency of an apparently inconsistent theory can be saved by modifying it ever so slightly. For example, the above inconsistent theories can be saved by saying that the theories refer to talking about sex, claiming men talk about sex more than women. Alternatively, the consistency can be saved if instead of referring to the average number of intercourses the theory refers to the median: since women-prostitutes have much more intercourses, the median among women is lower than then the median among men.

The claim that what someone says is not new is irrelevant, since many opinions are very old still and under dispute, and some of these disputes are very interesting. This is not so if the claim is made that the opinion put up for dispute is new and therefore deserves special attention. If you then object, saying that the assertion put forward not new, then, obviously, you bear the burden of proof; you have to show where the idea has been already presented. Note also that such a criticism still does not refer to the truth or falsity of the idea (to its truth-value, so-called) but rather to its novelty, and therefore to the special and new attention that novelty may require.

Finally, if you claim that the idea put up for debate is trivial, once again you bear the burden of proof; you have to show that the idea is already widely accepted or that it obviously follows from some widely accepted idea (or set of ideas). Note however that if a certain idea is trivial it follows that it is true, but since it is trivial the individual who presents it does not deserve special acclaim for having presented it. In any case, the claim that a statement is trivial is hardly interesting; the claim that a popular opinion that was presented as trivially true is false is much more exciting. Think, for example, of all the views about sex that were deemed trivially true a century ago that nowadays sound so weird.

Generalizations and Existential Statements

When reviewing disputed statements, you should check, for each statement, whether it is a generalization or an existential statement. A generalization is a statement that starts with "All", such as: "all ravens are black". Existential statements start with "there are" or "some" such as: "some ravens are black". These statements might be formulated negatively, for example instead of saying that all the raven are black one may say that there are no ravens that are not black, or that there are no non-black ravens; instead of saying that some ravens are black or that there exist black ravens, one may say that it is not the case that no raven is black or that not all raven are not black. (Classical and modern versions of logic both recognize these two equivalences. Classical logic also allows to infer from all ravens are black that some ravens are black. This is a mistake—a fallacy —and even obviously so, since all unicorns have one horn but there are no unicorns.)

A generalization might be true by virtue of their structure. "All ravens are ravens" is an example for this. A generalization might also be true by the meanings of its words. For example, all ravens are bird since ravens are birds by the very meaning of the words. Such statements are logically true. They should not be disputed. Except for logically true generalizations, theories cannot be proved. There is no way to prove that all the infinitely many ravens (including ravens in the future) are (and will be) black. When discussing such theories, the burden of proof rests on the opponent that should present a case that refutes them. By presenting ravens that are not black one can refute the theory that all the ravens are black. In other words, such a theory cannot be proved, but (in principle) can be refuted. The theory that all ravens are black is scarcely a theory. We can make it more of a theory by saying that every species has its own specific color, so that black and white ravens should count as different species, and so we should discuss not ravens but black ravens and white ravens. When we refute this theory about the colors of birds we can try to replace it by another.

So much for universal statements. The rule that applies for existential statements is the opposite. If one of the parties presents an existential statement, this party bears of burden of proof. The side that presents an existential statement should present examples that prove the statement (for example, pointing at some black raven in order to prove the statement that some ravens are black).

The previous few paragraphs belong to formal logic. They are not contestable. Their significance is for the theory of scientific argument; in science generalizations are called for as explanations. They are often called theorems, since scientific theories are often viewed mathematically when the question of their content is at issue (namely, what statement follows from what statement). This is important both when the explanatory power of a theory is at stake and when their truth value is. Explanatory power is examined when one generalization is supposed to follow from another, the question of the truth of the explanation is the question of what existential statement contradicts it. Such an existential statement follows from some empirical report that those who wish to refute it try to observe.

Things get complicated because by scientific tradition an observation statement is disregarded unless it is generalized. Yet the observation that entails the existential statement that contradicts the theory refutes it (and the failure to observe what it describes corroborates it) yet only its generalization is a candidate for scientific explanation.

You would expect that nevertheless researchers are not able to confuse a generalization or a theorem with its refutation or its negation that is existential. We have at least one such important example. It is called the second best theorem and it belongs to economics. It is this. Within economic theory we encounter theorems that tell you that optimizing one variable leads to optimizing another. And, naturally, we often wish the other quantity optimized. Suppose it is impossible to optimize the quantity whose optimization we are concerned with as we wish to optimize the other. It stands to reason that the way to do so is to get as near to the unattainable target as possible. The second best theorem is a refutation of this reasonable idea: there are important cases in economics where the optimization is not the nearest to the unattainable optimum.

The second-best theorem, thus is not a theorem, not a generalization, but a refutation; it is existential statement. Hence, it is not enough to prove it mathematically: one has to point at an example for it. This, of course, is what the discoverers of the interesting second-best theorem have done (R. G. Lipsey and K. Lancaster, "The General Theory of Second Best", *The Review of Economic Studies,* 24, 1956–1957, 11–32). Unless the presentation of an example for an existential statement is required, the task of disagreeing with a theory becomes too easy: everybody can say of any theory that it is false. Arguing against a theory is much harder and so it is much more of a challenge. This is why we have an elaborate system of rules about the challenge that criticizing a theory is, especially if the theory has already passed the first and most obvious tests. We are now coming to this, and thus the role of this book as a handbook is now on its way.

Chapter 5
Disputes About General Facts and Theories

Abstract Debates on answers to factual questions invite considering first what answer reduces the strangeness of the world, and perhaps also to what degree. Check which answer is simpler; of two theories that explain the same items, the simpler is usually preferred. Check also whether the theory under dispute successfully predicts previously unknown surprising facts or rather just explains known facts (the latter is much the easier one). Avoid debates with people who repeatedly change the wording of their assertions in response to refutations by applying ad hoc corrections to them, especially those who pretend that these corrections are mere clarifications. In general, adversaries who admit error frankly are preferable; more so those who admit error with no fuss.

Let us assume that agreement about the procedures (the burden of proof) is taken for granted, and the question under dispute is determined. Let us also assume that the question concerns the choice between universal theories (or sets of statements or the statement that is their conjunction). Next, as many answers to the question should be proposed, and some of them eliminated from the debate (tentatively, of course). Their merits and defects have to be debated one by one; the order in which they are debated is to be agreed upon. It is of extreme importance to realize that the order of discussion of the different answers is fluid. (It is easy to sabotage a debate by declaring the unpleasant answer so low a priority that it will never reach the top of the agenda.) And so the central task is now at hand, namely to resolve rationally the dispute over the answers: we want to find the right answer or at least to grade them. What is the procedure for that? To repeat, general skeptical considerations ensure that no final proof and no final refutation are possible of general facts and about informative theories.

Science has a rule that supposedly imposes refutations: a general fact that rests on repeated observations that contradicts a theory refutes it. In other words, the observation that contradicts a theory has priority over it. This rule presents the default option, but viewing it as hard-and-fast may cause unnecessary trouble; so, from time to time, researchers try to violate it while still remaining within the research tradition. On a rare occasion, researchers may admit the general fact and the conflict between it and the theory that they examine, and then put the fact aside for a while. As long as their research is interesting, people may pay attention to them; otherwise, they might find themselves scientifically isolated. Thus, atomic chemists in the early part of the nineteenth century admitted that there are cases of two different chemicals whose molecules contain the same atoms, which was contrary to their chemical atomism known as analytic chemistry. Yet they refused to give up their view and finally came up with the idea that not only the same atoms but also the same structure of the molecule is what makes for the identity of a chemical. This idea is known as stereochemistry. The exciting case was that of molecules that share even structure, except that one is the mirror image of the other—they are called isomers—yet one of them is a nutrient and the other is a poison. This was the discovery of Louis Pasteur that made him famous. The chemists of the earlier generation who had overlooked the refutation of analytic chemistry were rational as they admitted that they were in error, but it took them time to locate the error and so they continued the researches into analytic chemistry while admitting that they owed answers to their critics. Nowadays analytic chemistry is a respected sub-field of stereo-chemistry that sets limits to it. This is not the end of the story, since similar cases take place in quantum chemistry. This is just to say that research is endless and that at times in the absence of a solution to a problem, some researchers may circumvent it and pretend that it is solved.

Back to the question, how factual debates can be resolved. Since skeptical considerations ensure that no final proof and no final refutation are possible, what methods should be used for argumentation? Fortunately, we can find some help in psychology. In modern society, most people share a simple psychological trait: they change their opinions (at times with great efforts) in a way that makes the world look to them less strange. Therefore, when engaged in a dispute about factual generalizations and theories, the parties to the dispute may benefit from considering *which answer makes the world appear less strange.* If they do not agree whether situation A or B is stranger, then they can argue about this disagreement, along the same guidelines mentioned above. This procedure bears no logical difficulties, as the new dispute is about a dispute (it is on the meta-level). However, if one of the parties to a dispute sincerely suggests that they are not interested in which answer makes the world appear less strange, then possibly the debate about it will be fruitless. In this case, it makes sense to consider aborting it.

Let us observe certain circularity here. The supposed disposition to adopt views that reduce the strangeness or weirdness or oddity of the surrounding world is psychological and the supposition is that the disposition is not the outcome of conscious decisions. This disposition parallels the conscious effort of scientific researchers to explain the world. In particular, they try to explain both common phenomena like the blue color of the sky and the green color of grass. They also try to explain the odd phenomena, those that conflict with the opinions that they wish to replace by better ones. The better theories exclude the refutations of the older theories thereby reducing the strangeness of the world as it appears to them. We have said, the psychological disposition we describe is specific to the modern world, namely to science-oriented society. Nevertheless, even on the assumption that in science-oriented society science and psychology mirror each other, it is easier to discuss the psychological aspect of science than the rules of scientific research. For, science can be inaccessible to common people, and referring to their psychology is a way to keep out of the inaccessible aspect of science and of its rules of conduct.

Ad-hoc Theories

Philosophers of science, or rather methodologist, namely, students of the rules of scientific research, have observed several pitfalls that influence the degree of reasonability that we assign to considering a theory true, given the circumstances. These pitfalls are cases in which the theory renders the world stranger rather than less strange and so they are objectionable, both philosophically and psychologically.

The first and best-known pitfall is the admission of *ad hoc* changes to theories (scientific or commonsense). The Latin expression "*ad hoc*" means "for this"; thus, the difference between parliamentary standing and *ad hoc* committees is this: standing committees are permanent whereas the *ad hoc* are created for a purpose and disperse once their declared purpose is reached (usually after it had submitted a report on the issue for which the parliament instituted it). In science the term "*ad hoc*" applies to changes that one makes in a theory for a very limited purpose: just to circumvent refutations. The easiest way by which to achieve this is by declaring the unpleasant refuting cases mere exceptions. Consider the people who share a prejudice against Ruritanian people: they honestly judge all Ruritanian people stupid. Suppose that on some occasion they bump into a Ruritanian, Tom, whom they judge wise. Consequently, they change their view and assert that all Ruritanian people but Tom are stupid. On some other occasion they bump into another Ruritanian, Dick, whom they also judge wise. Consequently, they change their view yet again and take both Tom and Dick to be exceptions. This way it is possible to go on changing view whenever a counter-examples to a prejudices appears, without considering the option of dropping the prejudice altogether. This is what makes changes of this kind *ad hoc;* a theory that one alters to encompass corrections *ad hoc* thus becomes an increasingly *ad hoc* theory. Credence in it diminishes. A psychological explanation of this decrease in credibility refers to the above-mentioned psychological disposition of people in science-oriented societies to change their opinions in a way that makes the world look to them less strange. The tendency then is to doubt a theory that underwent many *ad hoc* modifications because—according to the psychological theory—it involves the highly unexpected event that all the exceptions to the initial theory have already been accidentally observed. The probability that the Ruritanian individuals we have met and no other Ruritanian individuals are wise, is anyway very small. Thus, the theory that has been repeatedly modified *ad hoc* tends to increase the strangeness of the world rather than decrease it.

This holds not only concerning a prejudice; it holds also for any received view, including a successful scientific explanation. For an example of a scientific theory, let us consider our psychological theory that says, in science-oriented societies people are disposed to change their opinions in order to reduce the strangeness of the surrounding world. Suppose we meet people who refuse to change their views despite their recognition of the evidence to the contrary. We will not say, the theory holds for all members of a science-oriented society except for Tom, Dick, and Harry. We will call them all dogmatists and change our psychological theory to say, the theory holds for all members of a science-oriented society except for dogmatists: all members of a science-oriented society change their views in order to make the world look less strange except for dogmatists. We then find people who change their views in order to agree with the last people they talked with; we can find such people with ease even in science-oriented societies. We will call these people fickle and alter our theory yet again, to say, unless people are dogmatic or fickle, they change their views so as to render the world look less strange. This reaction renders our psychological theory even more *ad hoc*. Suppose, however, that we say, some people find it easy to change their views and other people find it hard to do so, and we want to find out why. We then ask, do those who change their minds after deliberations have any criterion for doing so, or do they make these changes on a completely *ad hoc* basis? Of course, we can ask them. The result is very disappointing: people who are willing to change their minds and who do so fairly systematically do not know what makes them behave as they do, and they often offer poorly reasoned answers to this question. (The discovery of this phenomenon, and that it is common even among well-educated members of science-oriented societies, is known as the prospect theory of Daniel KahnemanandAmos Tversky; it won Kahneman Nobel Prize after Tversky died.) We may suggest that they do so in order to make the world appear less strange. Before we can examine this psychological theory and put it to empirical test, we have to decide clearly what kind of people we have in mind, or else it will be too easy to dismiss any possible counter-example that we may find by declaring that it is a seeming counter-example, as the individuals who deviate from our hypothesis are excluded as they are either fickle or dogmatic. Things can get worse: if we are asked, how we know that they are fickle or dogmatic, we can answer: we know this since they do not conform to our hypothesis. This will not enlighten anyone.

When people engaged in a debate change their view in an *ad hoc* manner, it makes sense to ask them if their last change is the final, and whether the next refutations will change their minds. We can ask people prejudiced against Ruritanian people, how many wise Ruritanian people will make them give up their opinion that the Ruritanian people are stupid. Of course, they may say that for this they need some statistics. This is reasonable, especially if they will admit that if statistically wisdom, defined any way they like, is as common among Ruritanian as among our native people, then they will change their opinion. This also will make them abide by our hypothesis. If they intend to cling to their opinion, and if it seems that they are going to save their opinion by applying more *ad hoc* changes, then there is little sense in continuing arguing with them. (In science-oriented societies dogmatism is permitted even if it may be frowned upon.) If they do agree that the last change was the final one, and if their previous changes were indeed *ad hoc*, then you may seek another refutation so as to conclude the debate. This, however, will not help if the question under dispute is vague, as is the case with our psychological hypothesis that enables us to dismiss all people who do not fit it as fickle or dogmatic. For, fickle and dogmatic people are very common (yes, even in science-oriented societies), and we have declared our hypothesis inapplicable to them. So we have to say to whom it clearly applies, so that we can try to criticize it in a reasonably clear fashion.

Note then that not any *ad hoc* change makes holding a theory unreasonable. Sometimes it helps render them clearer and better open to criticism. Science provides some examples of theories that were changed *ad hoc* and remained scientific. One famous example is the abnormality of water. The theory was, the volume of all kinds of matter expand when heated. But then it was discovered that water expands when it approaches freezing temperature (this is why ice floats on the sea) and the theory changed: the volume of all kinds of matter except for water expand when heated. (The maximum density of water occurs at 3.98 °C.) Another famous example comes from economics: the theory was: if price goes up, then the demand for it goes down and *vice versa*. But then Alfred Marshal discovered cases of what he called Giffen goods (after Robert Giffen, who first mentioned the possibility of such goods). A Giffen goods is any staple food of inferior quality. The poor consume it more than the rich; and so, when its price goes up/down, they are left with less/more money for superior substitutions, and therefore increase/decrease the demanded quantity of the staple food. So the new theory is: for all goods except for Giffen goods, if their price goes up, then the demand for them goes down. The question then is, how do we identify a Giffen good? This question was indeed answered conclusively. What then characterizes the cases of *ad hoc* changes that are desirable? The answer to this question must remain *ad hoc*: desirable *ad hoc* changes are those that help rather than impede critical discussion. In particular, they are not an endless process followed just for the sake of not allowing for the possible case that the theory in question is refuted; hence, desirable ad hoc changes may be quite rational. When do we stop examining whether such changes are rational? When the debate becomes frustrating.

The specific to scientific *ad hoc* hypotheses is that those concerned who are suspicious about them tend to test them. When the *ad hoc* hypothesis is corroborated, it ceases being *ad hoc* as the case of heat expansion of water shows. Newton's theory of gravity was twice rescued this way and twice the *ad hoc* hypotheses were corroborated very impressively. In one case in which it looked as if Newton's theory of gravity seemed refuted, an *ad hoc* hypothesis blamed the error on optical theory, and indeed, the hypothesis was corroborated and optical theory was altered (the correction is called the aberration theory of light; it takes into account the distortion due to the relative motion of source and recipient of light). When the new optical theory was considered the theory of gravity appeared to fit the facts. The second refutation was overcome by the assumption that an unnoticed planet caused a shift from the expected orbit of a distant planet. The location of the unnoticed planet was calculated on the assumption that Newton's theory of gravity is true. The unnoticed planet was then observed. The last refutation of Newton's theory of gravity was the perihelion motion of Mercury that is its secular motion. Secular means once in a century, namely, very slow. The planets nearest to the sun have their elliptic orbits rotate very slowly. Einstein knew of ad hoc hypotheses to account for this motion, but he took it seriously and refused to consider any *ad hoc* hypothesis for its rescue: he had argued that acting at a distance is impossible and so he looked for a radical change of the theory.

So when we exclude from our psychological hypothesis the dogmatist and the fickle *ad hoc* it remains for us to test this exclusion and thus either to refute it or to render it non-*ad hoc*. To do so we have to decide who is fickle and who is a dogmatist. How then do we do that? We suggest as the default option the same conventions for the degree of tolerance required of people so as to have an opportunity to change their minds in case they are or seem to be in error. The default option, note, is not always reliable: there may be theories with some degree of merit that deserve more attention before they are declared false. A standard example of such a situation (which many lack the physics background to understand) relates to a very advanced theory in quantum mechanics known as Dirac's equation for the electron. When Dirac hit upon it, he found easy evidence against it, yet the theory appealed to him so much that he decided to work on it some more and check the evidence against it after. And this decision proved to be right. Another famous example is Darwin's theory of evolution. When Darwin presented his theory of evolution, he claimed that hereditary traits are the average of the parents' traits. Critics of his view observed that hence traits created by mutation should disappear within a few generations. He ignored this criticism. The criticism was resolved only by the application of a variant of Mendel's theory, according to which the genes usually do not change during fertilization, except for cases of mutation. (Mendel's publication of his theory was earlier than Darwin's publication of his, but Darwin did not know about it. We will return to Darwinism and Neo-Darwinism shortly). To repeat, such things happen in science regularly, and many people love to dwell on them as they seem to justify dogmatism. Of course, we do not agree, especially since we do not think dogmatism needs justification: dogmatists do not look for it and they use it only in order to prove that they are not dogmatists. This may interest them very much; it does not interest us. We admit that we are all disposed towards dogmatism but counterbalance this with our proposed theory that in science-oriented societies there is also a disposition to change opinions. In any case we prefer to present techniques to limit our dogmatism, as we are doing just here.

Simplicity

A second pitfall refers to the degree of simplicity that different parties to a dispute assign to theories. As a matter of psychological fact, as well as a point of methodology that most philosophers of science admit, people, especially researchers, tend to prefer simpler explanations of facts over complicated ones. When several measurements of three measurements of a parameter on a grid appear as if they are more or less on a straight line, we tend to conclude that a straight line is going through these points. This line is not there: the conclusion that the data are on a straight line does not follow from observations, since there are infinitely many ways to draw a line through them (for example, an infinite number of wave functions coincide with them). The conclusion that the correct line is straight, then, is an extrapolation. Our hypothesis—namely, that we change our opinions in ways that make the world look to us less strange—explains the phenomenon as follows. The linear function is the least arbitrary. Once we allow any function, we have too many candidates. And so, the assumption that by sheer luck we hit on the right one does not reduce but rather raises the level of unexpectedness. And, to continue with our parallel, as the linear function is least arbitrary, says Karl Popper, it is most easily testable. Hence, if we test our hypotheses, we thereby render simplicity less a dogma and more a default option. Having a default option too is a dogma or a prejudice, so following Popper we prefer our default option to be anti-dogmatic.

A similar analysis applies to Occam's razor, which is the demand to eliminate unnecessary entities. People tend to disbelieve theories that they judge as multiplying entities needlessly. (We will come soon to the question, what is a need here.) the way our hypothesis explains this psychological phenomenon is the same way we explained simplicity: holding on stubbornly to defunct entities, to entities that have no longer any function, is at best a mere guess, and the assumption that such guesses comprise reliable sources of information increases the level of unexpectedness of experiences instead of reducing it. Note that many if not most superstitions assume the existence of unspecified entities that are responsible for the events that draw the attention of the superstitious. And so we should exclude from our psychological hypothesis not only the fickle and the dogmatist, but also the superstitious. This may sound excessively *ad hoc*, but as we specified from the start that our hypothesis describes on members of science-oriented societies, perhaps this is no added qualification and so not *ad hoc* in the least. It is hard for us to judge this matter. One way or another, whatever reason we offer, we must exclude such people, and so our theory that people are reasonable is modified *ad hoc* a bit too often to our taste. To narrow this undesirable aspect, many people declare superstition a form of prejudice and prejudice a form of dogma. These hypotheses are amply refuted, and you can try to compare people's conduct that looks more dogmatic than prejudicial or more superstitious than dogmatic, or *vice versa*. You will find that all these traits are conducive to arbitrariness, but in diverse ways: there are ever so many ways to be arbitrary, and the tough job is to come up with a simple one.

In some cases, the selection of the simplest explanation is obvious, and usually once it appears, it is not under dispute: very seldom do we have alternative hypotheses of equal degrees of simplicity. The above-mentioned straight line is one such example. But in some cases the selection is disputable, and this is the pitfall you should be aware of. History provides many examples. Consider the dispute about phlogiston. Wanting to know what makes some substances combustible, Georg Ernst Stahl said, combustibles can emit large quantities of phlogiston ("phlox" is the Greek for flame), which they do as they burn: combustion, he said, is the emission of phlogiston. Antoine Lavoisier then said, combustibles can absorb large quantities of oxygen, which they do as they burn. Combustion he said, is combination with oxygen, whether the oxygen compound is absorbed or emitted. For a while, there was evidence against the older theory and none against the new one. Nevertheless, some people found it very hard to let phlogiston go. They could, of course, consider Lavoisier's theory true, give up any refuted assertion about phlogiston, but still insist that while absorbing oxygen, combustibles also emit phlogiston. From the historical perspective, this case seems to demonstrate that advocates of the theory of the phlogiston were reluctant to abandon their view and failed to see that it makes the world more complex without gaining any explanation of unexpected phenomena. Psychologically, this is quite natural. The traditional theory seems to be simpler than the new one. Beware of this pitfall. One reason that some advocates of the theory of the phlogiston (especially the great Joseph Priestley) gave for their clinging to their view was that their theory was scientific, and scientific theories are proven and thus they cannot be overthrown. This led their opponent to call them dogmatists and argue that the theory of the phlogiston was never scientific; for a scientific theory cannot be refuted, and the theory of the phlogiston was. This is an example of extending a dispute about combustion to include the question of which views are and are not scientific. This extension demonstrates another pitfall. Keep focused and refuse to broaden the discussion, unless you find it interesting to do so or unless it helps develop the critical debate about it (as Popper has recommended).

Predictions vs. Explanations

Finally, the third pitfall that we wish to discuss rests on the difference between prediction and explanation. Predictions that come true are more convincing than explanations of known events. An obvious explanation for this fact is this. It is usually easier to create a new theory that successfully explains given events by offering generalizations than to predict correctly previously unobserved events, ones predicted only by the new theory. So the event of coming up with a theory that provides a new true prediction is more unexpected than coming up with a theory that provides a new explanation to past events. Consider an explanatory theory that also provides new testable predictions that turn out to be true. We do not expect a conjecture to be successful in predicting unexpected events. Hence, when a theory successfully predicts them, the assumption that the theory is true reduces the level of unexpectedness drastically, and so we tend to adopt it, at least for a while. As Einstein taught us to consider seriously the option that the new theory is nearer to the truth, this option is more attractive than the option that the new theory is true, and so it is preferred—even though we would prefer to have the truth rather than an increased approximation to it.

It follows then that in a dispute about an explanation (what is the true or at least the best explanation of the event A? Why did event A occur?), it makes sense to look for unexpected predictions that the competing explanations imply and to check if these predictions come true, and the less expected the better.

Conspiracy theories so-called provide an example for the difference between explanations of given unpleasant events and prediction of new ones. Conspiracy theories explain known events as caused by some unnamed and undescribed people who have profited from them. They avoid systematically issuing any prediction regarding future events, especially unexpected ones, as they avoid offering descriptions of the conspiring parties and of the exact profits that allegedly accrues from the unpleasant events that they explain. Conspiracy theories likewise avoid describing the ways they have caused the explained unpleasant events. So whenever you are involved in a dispute involving a conspiracy theory, ask the theory's proponents to provide such a description that should allow for a search for such a prediction. If they refuse, then they expose their theory as uninteresting as too easy to produce to fit the evens in question; if they agree, both parties can check whether the prediction that follows from their theory comes true. (Some such checking has to be successful, since some conspiracies do take place in one place or another, on one day or another.) The conspiracy theory is a form of superstition, except that most superstitious people refer in their explanations to some vague causes that may but need not be human, whereas conspiracy theories refer vaguely to some unspecified people. Indeed, their popularity rests on the ease with which one can conjure them with no fear of criticism, yet with a semblance of scientific character: they seem to enjoy the prestige of both magic and science; they also seem sophisticated and even clever, as any theory that claims to unmask a villain; except that its defect is that it does not unmask anyone in particular. We all begin our lives as morally naïve, and in contemporary science-oriented societies during our adolescence we lose our naiveté and tend to become cynical and reject all morality and all ethics. It is only if and when we move away from this second stage of adolescence that we face as adults the problems of morality and of ethics. Conspiracy theory aficionados are out of the first stage and so they consider themselves sophisticated, even though they are stuck in the second stage.

Another example is the dispute about the so-called Bible Code. The claim in question is that somehow the Bible contains all possible (significant) information. This is no answer to any specific question, let alone an interesting one. Let this ride. Efforts were repeatedly made to find in the Bible the latest scientific theories and the latest significant political information and similar data, or simply some impressive major event such as the assassination of a leading political leader. People who advocate this idea have repeatedly tried to show that a series of prophecies can be "read between the lines" or revealed by selective reading of words or letters. The favorite example is reading a certain letter in the biblical text, then skipping a certain number of letters, reading another letter, skipping the same number of letters, reading the next letter, and so on repeatedly—in effort to find one example of this kind that displays one message or another. Sooner or later, this way bound to construct some text that makes some sense as a message, allegedly demonstrating foreknowledge. Allegedly, the existence of such texts is unexpected, except on some supposition about the power of sacred texts. Simple statistical considerations point at the enormous number of possible text messages to be found by following this kind of procedure; statistical analysis suggests then that any case that answers the aficionado's expectation is a mere coincidence. Therefore, any dispute on whether the existence of such textual messages demonstrates the sanctity of sacred texts or is due to a mere coincidence that signifies nothing can be easily resolved by seeking predictions. The former explanation (that the messages demonstrate the sanctity to sacred texts) implies that similar messages should not be revealed in secular text, such as novels or even telephone books, not to mention texts sacred to other religions. The latter explanation (that the messages are the result of highly probable coincidence) predicts that secular text will include similar messages. And, indeed, the latter was found empirically.

The dispute about the Bible Code so-called illustrates a risky pitfall: it is all too easy to find regularities in any sufficiently large data-base (Bernoulli's law). These regularities might seem unexpected, even though careful calculations suggest that they result from probable coincidences. Hence, theories that explain them do not reduce the strangeness of the world. And as far as science is concerned, the situation is even worse: scientific explanations deal only with repeatable events. Random evens like some unusual correlations are unrepeatable, although in some sense they are indeed repeatable. The simplest case is what is known as the gambler's fallacy. A gambler who sees an unusual series of events, say a long series of throws of a coin that turn up to be all heads may reason thus: since the longer a series of heads is, the less likely it is, the likelihood is that the next throw will be a tail. Or the gambler may reason that since he has observed so many heads, it is more likely that the next throw will be a head. This reasoning is called Laplace's rule of succession as the great theoretician Laplace has offered it, though in a different context. Trying to justify projections he argued that since we have observed the sun rise for at least three millennia, it is almost certain that it will rise tomorrow. Very oddly, all thinkers who tried to justify science tried to prove that the sun will rise tomorrow, even though no one doubted it; and then science claimed that one day the sun will explode, we do not know when, but possibly even tomorrow. Back to our gambler. If the coin that gamblers put their hopes on are thrown randomly (by flipping them), then given a series of heads, no matter how long, the chance that the next throw can depend on its predecessors is but an illusion. We will discuss all this in more detail in the next chapter. Before that, in the next section, we will discuss another example of the phenomenon of statistical illusion.

Before that, let us suggest the following observation. Our psychological hypothesis may be true or false, we do not know. Nothing rests on this, and we mention that it is a useful tool, no more than that: debates are possibly tools for convincing people, so that the more persuasive party has the better likelihood to win. As stated above, though, we hope that this is not the aim of all debates; we focus on the educational role of debates, on those conducted with the aim of coming as close to the truth as possible, in part by weeding out troublesome errors.

The Theory of Evolution or Evolutionism

To repeat, parties to a dispute about factual generalizations and about theories may benefit from considering what answer makes the world look less strange. The classical arguments in favor of an explanatory theory are unexpected empirical predictions that follow from the theory and are supported by observations that contradict its extant rivals or at least do not follow from them. Since the predicted empirical phenomena were initially counter-expected, the theory explains more than its rivals, and thus its use turns the initially counter-expected phenomena into expected ones and thus the exercise reduces the strangeness of the apparent world. However, this process is not the only way to reduce perceived strangeness. The discussion about Darwinian evolutionary theory, as well as its neo-Darwinian heir, can serve as examples for an alternative.

Darwinism comes to answer to the question, what is the origin of species? What explains the variety of observed species? Prior to Charles Darwin, leading naturalists considered the variety of species inexplicable, or explicable, if at all, as expressions of divine intervention (which amounts to the same). Evolutionism is not the invention of Charles Darwin: it is ancient. Also, his grandfather Erasmus Darwin was an evolutionist. Evolutionism rests on the intuitive idea that members of some species resemble members of another species. It does not explain the origin of species, namely the rise of new species. Darwin's immediate predecessor, Charles Lyell, did try to explain the rise of new species; his idea was unsuccessful although it was historically important, as it put the problem on the research agenda and as it was the first theory that referred to ecosystems, an item central to the evolutionism of Darwin. By his theories as well as by those of his heirs, the variety of species is explicable as a natural process: changes occur (accidentally or in any other way) and most of them vanish; those changes that survive do so because they improve the likelihood of survival of the animals in which they occur. And they do so because the new sort of animal fits its environment, its ecosystem, better or worse; those that survive fit their environments well enough to live long enough to reproduce. The question is what is well enough? Answer: animals compete for eco-niches, and among competing individuals only those that fit better survive long enough to have offspring. This then suffices also to create new species as Darwin redefined the concept. (Unlike Aristotle, and the multitude of his heirs, Darwin considered a species not as a set of typical characteristic but as a set of animals liked by blood relationship. Thus, according to Aristotle, animals in two continents that have the same typical characteristics will count as one species, whereas Darwin considered them as two different species. Thus, he said, had white-skinned and black-skinned humans not shared offspring, he would count them as two species; the presence of mulattos keeps the human race one.)

Darwinism is hardly refutable. This is so since we do not know whether a new trait is conducive to survival or not, since quite possibly it is detrimental to survival but is associated with a trait that is conducive to survival. (The paradigm case is sickle cell anemia that is decidedly detrimental to survival yet it comes with inborn immunity to malaria that is.) Since refutability is the possibility of finding counterexamples, to find out whether a theory is refutable it is necessary to consider an experiment, to begin with a mere thought experiment, that can in principle be performed with the possible outcome that might make adherents to that theory admit error. Suppose that geologists find several geological layers that contain petrified bones in the opposite order than the one expected by Darwinism (for example, remains of humans in the deeper geological layer than those of their ancestor). How can such a find comprise a refutation of Darwinism? Of course, the question is not easy, since most people will find this kind of find hardly thinkable. Yet the disappearance of dinosaurs and the appearance of small mammals afterwards is not vastly different from the result envisaged here. Indeed, with some ingenuity, one can conjecture an evolutionary process that hit a brick-wall and that has only some fossils to testify to its initial occurrence. The literature includes many conjectures of this kind. The evolutionist framework within which such considerations take place is still not testable, as it will absorb any result of such a test.

Not only is evolutionary theory itself scarcely refutable; most of the explanations presented through this framework are too. For example, it allows for the explanation of the giraffe's long neck by assuming that the long neck was developed accidentally among several giraffes but those giraffes gained a survival advantage in comparison with the other giraffes (since they could eat food available on tall trees). As a result, their rate of reproduction increased, while the short-necked giraffes became extinct because the two kinds of giraffe compete for the same eco-niche. This explanation is irrefutable. Thus, were there no long-necked giraffes, we would not see it as a refutation of Darwin evolution theory. Moreover, some observations show—not unexpectedly—that the giraffe's long neck has some obvious disadvantages. (Famously, every change has both advantages and disadvantages.) The disadvantage is that the long neck makes it hard for the giraffe to drink water and so while drinking it is vulnerable. We cannot comparatively assess the relative advantages and disadvantages of long necks. The mere existence of long necks, though, suggests that they are more advantageous than disadvantageous, of course. Still, we somehow do find this argument regarding the giraffes as a rational argument in favor of Darwinism, since Darwin's evolution theory reduces the level of strangeness of the world by explaining how the variety of species can be explained as accidental. To repeat, prior to Darwin, the variety of species and more so the similarities and the changes in this variety were left unexplained. Darwin shows that each such a case is given to a possible explanation as a process of accidental changes where the fittest survive. Following this mode of explanation, the variety of species as such becomes less surprising, although the details of the variety are still surprising and are still awaiting detailed explanation. Thus, although Darwinism is scarcely refutable, it is a powerful system within which to state refutable hypotheses and test them, including such hypotheses as this about sickle cell anemia and about giraffe's peculiarities. (The ideas available as frameworks for scientific explanations are known as metaphysical or intellectual frameworks for explanatory hypotheses.)

Refutable predictions then are only one kind of reducing strangeness, one kind of such arguments; it is the strongest kind, though. Another kind, as the discussion about Darwinism indicates, is offering some intellectual frameworks that turn the inexplicable into hopefully explicable, or by showing that inexplicable phenomena are inexplicable due to some unspecified accidental causes, so that though they are individually inexplicable, they are explicable as series of phenomena.

What kinds of arguments are relevant for criticizing Darwinism? Several arguments pointed at cases that allegedly cannot be explained by a theory that follows Darwin's explanatory scheme. The eye is presented as paradigm case. Repeated claims have been made that the eye is so complex that it cannot be developed by one change (especially not an accidental change), and it cannot develop in stages, since in all the stages leading to the appearance of a complete eye, it was useless for survival or perhaps even more detrimental to the survival of an organism than useful for it. Whether this or similar arguments are valid or not lies beyond the scope of this handbook. All we can say here is this. Obviously, this kind of argument is rational, and so it is one that requires further study.

The case of religious arguments against evolution is very different. A famous example is the claim that Darwinism is false since it is inconsistent with Scriptures. This argument ignores the idea that Darwinism makes the world less strange (or assumes that any inconsistency with Scriptures makes the world stranger). Following our recommendation in the introduction of this handbook, we can hardly expect current debates about the status of Scriptures to be fruitful. In this case it makes sense to avoid for now all such arguments as a default option. Indeed, many religious biologists feel this way about the matter. (Others reinterpret Scriptures to accord with Darwinism, a possibility that greatly appealed to Darwin himself.)

Global Warming

We will end this chapter by reviewing the debate about global warming. This is a debate about factual question, and therefore can serve as a test case for the suggestions presented in this chapter.

The questions under dispute are: Does the word become warmer? If so, why, and what is the best way to prevent it?

Most students of global warming agree about most of the relevant facts. The world is getting increasingly and significantly warmer since the beginning of the twentieth century to date. This is a trend that will probably not desist overnight. One of the main reasons for this trend is the burning of fossil fuel that humans activate. This makes most of the students of global warming issue repeated warnings: they declare that if this trend goes on, the damages to the human society will be unbearable and probably irreversible. Now this set of agreed upon assumption that raise worry about global warming and invite some action, is attenuated by another set of agreed upon factual information. The globe undergoes warming and cooling repeatedly and for thus-far unknown reasons and with thus-far unpredictably. This raises the suspicion that there is nothing that humanity can do about the danger. Quite a few of the students of global warming, and some of them are members of conservative think-tanks, disagree with the majority of the students of global warming. They claim that (1) the warming during the twentieth century is within normal temperature variations, and there were several periods in the past where the temperatures were as high as they today; and (2) the contribution of human to the global warming is quite marginal.

One of main arguments of the conservative think tanks is the following: Researchers have proposed several models for the global climate, but unfortunately each of these models have failed to predict climate changes. In other words, all the models have been refuted, and we have no model that explains satisfactorily the known facts, let alone one that in addition stands up to new tests. Therefore, there is no rational basis for the predictions that global warming will continue and cause a global catastrophe. Against this argument we suggest to consider the following question.

Consider the theory that the globe become ever warmer for quite a while, that this trend will continues so that human society will suffer enormous damages; consider also the theory that no big risk is to be expected; which of these two theories makes the world stranger? The conservative think-tanks people do not present a theory that explains the observed climatic change, and as such they do not reduce the strangeness of world. They present an existential statement to the effect that some observed cases do not agree with every known climate model. Indeed, the students of climate change keep modifying these models, and these modifications are still somewhat *ad-hoc*, but still these are the best theories we have to apply when we consider which theory reduces the strangeness of the world.

There are other relevant considerations to be taken into account when reviewing global warming, such as costs of the following two scenarios—the scenario that global warming continues and the damages to the human society will be as severe irreversible as the students of climate changes predict, versus the scenario that we will drastically cut the pollution, and eventually will discover that there was no need for this measure. We will return to this kind of consideration in Chap. 9.

Chapter 6
Disputes About Statistical Generalizations

Abstract Discussing differences between samples, remember that within large samples, even a small difference might be statistically significant yet not necessarily interesting or relevant to the concern that has prompted it. So you may still want to inquire whether any given difference is worth discussing. Prior to debating assertions that explain certain event, investigate first the assertion that the event in question is due to a mere accident. Avoid debates on causality (unless your concern is philosophical). Discussing the degree to which the appearance of one variable makes us expect the appearance of another usually suffices.

Many disputes refer to statistical generalizations, such as:

1. The use of cellular phones causes cancer.
2. Most students forget most of what they have learned for an exam a short time after it.

Such statements do not present strict generalizations. Rather, they are statistical. They describe what happen often, but not necessarily always. To be more precise, considering any generalization of the form, if a then b, we expect every appearance of a to be accompanied by b; not so in statistical generalizations. When we say, Ruritanian people are wise, we are imprecise; we mean adult Ruritanian people, and we mean usually, or most of them. The first example above says that those who use cellular phones often enough are more likely to suffer from cancer than those who do not. And even that is not precise enough: to be testable it has to correlate the length of time of the use of the cellular phone with the degree of increased probability of suffering from cancer within this or that time period. Often enough statisticians do not specify these correlations and expect their empirical finds to tell them that. This is a cause of many statistical errors. Still, what matters to us here is that a critic who says, here is a person glued to a cellular phone and not suffering from cancer has not offered a criticism of the hypothesis, although if a critic says, here is a worker who fell from a scaffolding to the ground and was not harmed does refute the (true) hypothesis that declares such an event impossible.

Likewise, the second example above says that most but not necessarily all students forget most but not necessarily all of what they learn for an exam soon afterwards. Indeed, many teachers endorse this assertion, and they estimate that only about, say, one tenth of the material memorized is remembered, and so they demand ten times more than they estimate that students need to remember. (In truth, as Einstein noted, you need not remember what you can look up; just learn how to look up the information you may need.) Moreover, we know that this does not hold for students with total recall. We can, of course, qualify our second example above for students to exclude those with total recall. This may defy the purpose of this statement. The purpose is to replace exams with some other means for motivating students to study, and here ignoring any kind of students may defeat this purpose.

In brief, statistical generalizations are neither confirmable nor refutable by single examples to the contrary. This is contrary to the case of existential statements. Consider "some cellular users suffer from cancer". Most people will say, it is confirmed by merely one example of a person who uses cellular phone and suffers from cancer. This is highly questionable: in the modern world many people take vitamins and most of those who take vitamins do not suffer from cancer, and yet the existence of (many) people who take vitamins and do not suffer from cancer does not lead to agreement with the claim that vitamins prevent cancer. This is perhaps the greatest difference between popular acclaim or reputation and scientific tests. You may think that this is obvious, yet it is not. The most popular philosophical theory is one that Carl G. Hempel has advertised, according to which every case of a person who takes vitamins and does not suffer from cancer corroborates the theory that taking vitamins prevents cancer. Also, a college that admits only students that belong to the top one percent and whose graduates belong to the top ten percent is said to have done a good job. This is how statistics can mislead: one looks at results instead of comparative results. Thus, at the very least, the existential statement that does confirm our suspicion about cellular phone causing cancer is that people who use them are more likely to get cancer than others. And Popper says, this is not enough: Statisticians should look at those cases under which cellular phones should make cancer most likely to show that they do not; or they should look at the cases least likely to show that they do.

This is common sense. Nevertheless, objections from commonsense may appeal to some hidden causal links. To repeat our caution, we do not know what causes are. Let us wave this objection in favor of commonsense causal talk. This is tricky, and for very commonsense reasons: we usually do not spell out our causal assertions. We say, the king was beheaded, meaning he was executed and so he died. But there is more to it, said Karl Popper. Consider the commonsense example of causality that since David Hume's discussion of causality became the paradigm case. The stone thrown at the window shattered the glass. So the flying stone caused the glass to break. Hume argued that we do not see this causation. We overrule him here in the name of commonsense. So consider a quarry, where stones fly all the time. Windowpanes made for quarries are made to withstand flying stones. Suppose a windowpane in a quarry is shattered. We do not blame a flying stone then. Rather, we suggest that there was an air-bubble in the glass and that accidentally a flying stone hit it just where the air-bubble was. Again we see that commonsensically we omit much relevant information on the assumption that we are understood anyway. If we are mistaken, then we may repeat the information more explicitly. We do that also when a debate requires it, namely, when we disagree about what are the relevant conditions for an event; for, to repeat, we never know. In contemporary western society this ignorance is part and parcel of commonsense. And if need be, we say so explicitly. As in science all this is commonsense and more emphatically so, in discussions that belong to natural science it is now more customary than in common situations to avoid talking about causality and to talk about putative laws of nature instead.

So to find out about cellular phones and cancer, at the very least it is wise to avoid talk about causality and instead to compare the occurrence of cancer in the population of heavy users and of non-users of cellular phones. In this sense, statistical generalizations are similar to strict generalizations. You cannot confirm the generalization that "all cellular-phone users suffer from cancer" by presenting one or even by many cellular-phone users who suffer from cancer. Likewise, finding many cellular-phone users who suffer from cancer does not confirm the rule that "most cellular-phone users suffer from cancer."As the rule refers to infinitely many cellular-phone users (including those who will be users in the future), there is no way we can assess all of them. However, contrary to strict generalization, obviously the statement "most cellular-phone users suffer from cancer" cannot be refuted by one example of a cellular-phone user not inflicted with cancer. By saying that most (contrary to all) cellular-phone users suffer from cancer, the statement allows for some cases of healthy cellular-phone users. To refute a statistical generalization, not to mention comparative ones, the analysis of statistical data is needed, as well as some careful statistical calculations.

How then is it possible to criticize rationally the statement that the use of cellular phone causes cancer? Here are some suggestions.

Whenever possible, avoid speaking about causality; rather, speak about what will happen if one uses a cellular phone. Philosophers have been discussing causality for ages, and they are far from any agreement about the matter at hand. Suppose cellular-phone users tend to suffer from cancer at levels higher than the population average. Does this mean that their use of cellular phones is the cause of the cancer? If so, why do some people who use cellular phones not suffer from cancer? And is our biology not also a cause? These are complicated questions, and it is easy to shake the faith that causality is obvious. True, we do observe causality. (Hume said that we do not, but he employed a perception theory that is refuted over a century ago.) Consider this: when we see in a movie a sequence that defied causality, we are incredulous without even thinking about it. Yet at times our strongest intuitions can be curbed by simple commonsense. This is so well-known that we like commonsense teased. Thus, magic tricks are examples of our senses tell us that we see violations of causality and we know that this is not the case. Philosophers who insist on the veracity of our sensations promise to say how they insist on this despite magic tricks and, worse, despite sense illusions. They do not, since they cannot. They cannot even try.

Our example from stones that cause window-panes in quarries to break shows that the cause of an event can be very complex, and that we ignore many items in our description of a causal course of events as belonging to the context and we single out one item that is rare in the context and say, this is the cause of that event.

Except for expert philosophers (of certain schools), disputing parties to causal discussions are most likely not interested in all this. In order to keep to their interest, we can replace the discussion of causality with a discussion of the following question that is detached from causality: (all other things being equal) does the use of cellular phones increase the probability of suffering from cancer?

Logically speaking, as a single singular statement contradicts a strict generalization, so a single proper sample contradicts a statistical generalization. It is important to speak of a proper sample, since the selection rules that go into the sampling method may easily guarantee that the sample will agree with the statistical generalization in question, and equally easily it will contradict the generalization—as you will. This is so common, it has a technical name: it is called a biased sampling. (Most statistical evidence that you meet is likely to be biased, especially ones referred to in commercial advertisements.) This should not annoy you; rather you should center on the central question at hand. That question is, what sample is proper and how do we find it? There is no general answer to this question. To avoid bias, researchers try to collect a random samples. If someone declares the sample biased by criticizing the sampling method, then the criticism is used for a new sampling. For example, if one claims that the sample is of literate people and that this makes it biased, then we can seek a sample some of whose people are literate and some not. You may think this example bizarre, but it is not in the least: diets of literate people are known to differ from those who are not, and food is known to contribute to cancer. You may still refuse to take our example as reasonable and as why should the food of literate people differ from that of illiterate people as far as cancer is concerned. We need not be able to answer this question for our example to be reasonable: any objection to sampling should be used for a new sampling the way we have described in our example. But as it happens we have the answer to this objection: as we know, processed food is more easily available in advanced societies, and their populations are more often literate than those in other societies; hence, literate populations consume processed food much more frequently than illiterates, and processed food is a standing suspect to blame for the rise in incidents of cancer in contemporary industrial society.

Every sampling method can be suspect, and every suspicion, we say, is properly taken care of if it leads to repetition of the test with some new, appropriate sampling method. This is naturally very tedious. To avoid this, scientific researchers prefer running a controlled experiment. Subjects (people who agree to partake in the experiment) sampled as randomly as is possible are divided into two samples, again as randomly as is possible; subjects in one sample, say, use cellular phones, and subjects in the other sample (the control sample so-called) avoid using them. If after a certain (predetermined) time, the frequency of cancer in the first sample is indeed higher than the frequency of cancer in the second sample, a statistical test is applied to calculate if the difference is statistically significant. (A difference is deemed statistically significant when it is unwise to overlook it. Ignoring the difference between the two samples is allowed if it is deemed sufficiently small, or if it is very high but deemed due to a freak accident. The calculation often comes to show that the probability of a freak accident is very low, so that we may ignore it.) Such experiments did take place indeed, finding that in the population, no difference exists between those who use cellular phones and those who avoid using them, and therefore the difference that was found in the experiment between the two samples' cancer rates was merely coincidental. This, however, is debatable, and critics try to show by sophisticated means that the use of cellular phones is dangerous. For this they need a theory that should help them prove their point empirically. For example, both parties to the dispute agree that certain cancers are irrelevant to the test and other cancers are very relevant to it. This may help conclude the debate faster. Suppose that they argue about the proper use of the instrument: suppose they agree that holding the instrument in a certain way as in taking self-photos is the possible culprit. They then can repeat the experiment with one sample using the cellular phones but no selfies and others taking selfies often enough.

Whenever possible, this method is indeed the best one to resolve disputes. Note, however, the following pitfalls.

First, as was already mentioned in Chap. 2, a difference may be significant but not interesting. When the samples are large, even small differences become statistically significant, and yet they may not be interesting. If, for example, the difference between the two samples under discussion is just one per cent or one per thousand or lower (in measuring rates of presence of medications or of poisons such as air-pollutants, we often discuss parts per million) then even if this difference turns out to be statistically significant, you may say that you are not interested in such a small increase in risk. As mentioned above, a difference is significant if the probability is small that the event appeared by sheer accident. So when a difference in samples is significant, it makes sense to assume that a difference in the same direction holds in the population at large but still claim that being small, the difference as such is not interesting.

Second, the experiment rests on the assumption that the only relevant difference between the two samples is that the subjects in one sample, say, use cellular phones and in the others refrain from doing so. This assumption might always be challenged and then it found problematic—especially when the samples are small. Allegedly, assigning the subjects to each of the two samples randomly may solve this problem. But when the samples are small, the random division of one sample to two may not be sufficiently adequate. So the designers of the experiment usually see to it that the two samples are equal in the parameters that are known (or suspected) to be relevant: say, the same proportion of men and women, the same distribution of ages, etc. Obviously, the designers have to decide which parameters are relevant since they cannot refer to all possible parameters (there are infinitely many of them). They rely on their theories and assumptions regarding what is relevant to the issue under research. (In our example the issue is of suffering from cancer.) But, clearly, researchers are of necessity in the dark regarding all the possibly relevant parameters, since the theories and assumptions that they rely on might be erroneous (and to repeat, we can never be assured that we are free of all error).

History is full of such examples. Every occupational disease qualifies if it was hard to locate, and every poison that evaded observation. Even in common medical treatment this happens regularly. For centuries, children sensitive to lactose were given milk-rich diets; stomach-ulcer patients were given diets rather than medications, even after the discovery of antibiotics; they were instructed to take it easy on the supposition that their irritability had caused their ulcer rather than that the ulcer had made them irritable. And then it turned out that contrary to received opinion, cancer is due to a microbe that is able to live in acid environments. The paradigm-case still is that of thalidomide, the medication first marketed in 1957 in West Germany that was found immensely effective against headaches. As it turned out soon, pregnant women who used it gave birth to deformed offspring. Consequently, these days the wrappings of many medications bear a label warning pregnant women against using them.

Third, in many cases, ethical considerations prevent conducting possibly enlightening experiments. The case under our present discussion may serve as an example. If researchers seriously suppose that using cellular phone might largely increase the probability of suffering from cancer, then we may consider unethical to assign randomly some of the subjects to the sample that uses cellular phones. In the present case we may say, most people use these instruments anyway, so that the experiment may cause no damage. This raises different questions that we will skip here, observing that at times these are answerable adequately, at times not.

In the latter case, as in cases where practical problems in issuing experiments are impractical, we may wish to resolve disputes by other means. Possibly, the study of extant data may help, possibly patients who have nothing to lose and much to gain are willing to volunteer and undertake risk, and so on. More generally, whenever desired factual data (from controlled experiments or otherwise) is unavailable, parties to a dispute can still argue on the basis of some known data. They should try to figure out which theory that explains the data makes the data (and the world) less unexpected. Considering the case under discussion, for example, one may start by finding the frequency of cancer among cellular-phone users in general, and compare it against the frequency of cancer in the entire population.

Suppose the frequency of cancer among cellular-phone users is indeed found to be higher than the frequency of cancer in the population at large. This observation does not close the dispute about whether or not the use of cellular phones increases the probability of cancer. There are two reasons for this.

First, as long as no controlled experiment was issued, the difference between the samples (regarding the frequency of cancer) might result from some other differences between them (rather than the specific difference of cellular phone usage). We have mentioned one example already. For another example, it might be the case that city-dwellers are more likely than the entire population both to use cellular phones and to suffer from cancer due to the higher degree of pollution in urban and rural environments. The higher rate of cancer among the cellular-phone users therefore might be the result of living in cities, rather than of using cellular phones. Of course, it is possible to check this hypothesis and filter the data in order to hold constant the frequency of the subjects living in cities (in both samples). But this was just one possible hypothesis; many more factors might be relevant. However, since we do not have a satisfactory etiology of cancer, that is, since we do not have a good theory about the factors related to cancer, we cannot hold constant all the ones that the different parties to the dispute may agree to consider reasonably relevant.

(This last paragraph, incidentally, shows that efforts to ignore causality, even when successful, may be very partial: ignoring some troublesome ideas does not always make them go away.)

Second, the samples may be not representative and thus it may mislead: the observed difference between the samples might be accidental and not reflect the situation in the population at large. In that case the difference in samples does not hold in the entire population. The reason for the higher of frequency of cancer among the cellular-phone users (relative to the average frequency in the whole population) then is a result of a coincidence. (Statistical theory tells us that almost for sure among many samplings, some results will happen to be biased no matter how careful and how correct the sampling methods are. This is called Bernoulli's law. The trouble is, this law does not help us spot the error.) Allegedly, we can calculate the probability that the observed phenomenon is misleading, and if this probability is very low we may reasonably conclude that the explanation according to which the difference is coincidental is improbable. This reasoning, though proper, has a flaw, and one that at times shows up most forcefully. It is this. The assumption behind this reasoning is that events with a low probability very rarely or never appear in any sample although plenty of them do occur now and then. For example, guess a phone number and think of the name of a person. The probability of that person having that phone number is obviously very low since there are many alternative options here. But because just many people have phone numbers, at sometimes such a guess will come true for sure. (This, again, is an example of Bernoulli's law.)

One way to avoid this pitfall is to issue predictions. For example, following the hypothesis that the use of cellular phones increases the probability of suffering from cancer, you may predict that higher cellular phone invoices will be strongly correlated with the frequency of cancer. Only after issuing the prediction you should check the data. And if after several such trials you do not find the predicted correlation, you may reasonably conclude that the hypothesis is (tentatively) refuted.

As we have noted in the previous chapter, people want theories to reduce the strangeness of the world. When a theory predicts an otherwise improbable event, and this event turns out to be observed, the theory reduces the strangeness of the world simply by rendering the event probable. But observing such events does not tell the whole story. It also makes sense to consider the accepted theories that are relevant to the dispute. In the example under discussion, it makes sense to consider the accepted theories about cellular phone radiation and the influence of such radiation on the human body. (Radiation is assured to have ill-effect on us if it is hard, short-wave, such as x-rays and if it is in high intensity; cellular phones use low-intensity soft or long-wave radiation.) Since these theories imply that cellular phone radiation is too week to increase the probability of cancer, then accepting the idea that the use of cellular phone does increase the probability of cancer implies that these theories are false, and such a conclusion increases the strangeness of the world. Indeed, we should be open to considering data that seem to refute theories, but when the theories under discussion have been well tested, we should ask for strong evidence in order to act on the found refutation. Remember: evidence never impose the view that theories that conflict with it are false. This depends on your decision, and here we do suggest that you use commonsense, as here its use is vital.

Accidental Patterns

To repeat, one of the main risks involved in discussions of statistical generalization is that the observed facts that "lead" to the generalization under discussion may be accidental. That children are often in error when they generalize indiscriminately is well known. The following pitfall is not. Beware of it. When a data set includes relatively few cases with many features, it is easy to find patterns in them. Each of these patterns may look reasonable, but not all of them. They are then results of the enormous number of possible patterns. Since there are so many possible patterns, some of them turn out to hold by sheer accident.

For an example, consider the following table:

A	B	C	D	E	F	G	H	I	J	K	L	M	N	O
9	8	2	8	9	2	3	2	1	7	6	3	4	2	T
3	8	0	7	5	2	6	2	5	8	4	4	3	1	T
3	2	4	0	9	6	5	4	1	8	2	2	8	9	F
1	1	6	7	2	4	7	1	9	6	7	5	8	1	F
7	0	3	6	6	2	2	5	4	6	9	6	6	6	T
0	5	9	5	5	2	3	7	6	5	1	6	8	7	F
7	2	3	6	9	2	6	8	5	3	4	2	3	8	T
3	1	4	4	2	6	8	4	4	4	8	8	1	3	T
5	7	3	4	0	7	8	3	4	7	6	3	8	9	F
3	1	0	3	6	9	9	2	9	2	6	1	6	8	F
4	7	4	0	9	4	4	8	4	9	2	0	1	1	T
6	4	1	9	1	1	7	7	0	6	5	3	2	4	T
1	5	0	8	2	0	5	5	0	1	4	1	7	2	T
1	7	8	1	7	3	0	2	1	1	4	2	0	1	F
2	6	4	8	1	0	7	0	1	0	9	1	6	3	T

This table includes 15 columns and 15 rows. Such data are quite common in medical research (alternative medicine included) where the number of subjects is quite limited (especially in the study of rare diseases), while the number of qualities measured for each subject is quite large. So assume that this is indeed a table of some medical research, where each column denotes a specific medical feature or measurement, and each row denotes a particular subject.

Now, all the values in this table are random numbers. (They were created by an Excel Random function.) And yet, in spite of the fact that they are random, it easy to find allegedly interesting patterns. For example, one pattern is the following:

The value in column O is F if-and-only-if the value in column M is 8.

The accuracy of this rule is almost 90% – it holds for 13 out of the 15 subjects. Still, since the data are random, obviously this rule is not valid: in a repeated experiment there will be no trace of it. It therefore obviously makes no sense to use it in order to issue predictions for new cases.

How can we avoid this pitfall? Two methods are recommended; we have already mentioned them:

1. To test the validity of a theory, issue predictions for new cases.
2. Check the consistency of the suggested theory with your other ideas.

Debates About Healthy Diets

We will end this chapter by reviewing the debate about the question: what is the recommended healthy diet? This is a debate that both scientists in nutrition science and common people are interested in for obvious reasons.

As we explained above, the most valid method to check this question is by running controlled experiments. Several groups of people are selected randomly, each group eats another diet under consideration, and after several years the health of each group is tested. Unfortunately, this is easier said than done. People may not follow the diet instructions when they eat at home, and they may drop from their group because they dislike the food. And indeed the number of successful controlled experiments in this field is quite low.

The alternative, less accurate method is looking for correlations between various diets and health of the people that eat these diets. Many research surveys followed this method. But due political and self-pride interests many of these research have doubtful validity (for a detailed description of these researches see Nina Teicholz, *The Big Fat Surprise: Why Butter, Meat and Cheese Belong in a Healthy Diet*, 2014).

It is easy to find some counter examples for any recommended healthy diets. For example, a popular recommendation is to reduce saturated fat. But the Inuit and the Maasai eat food that contains a lot of saturated fat yet they suffer from heart diseases less than people in the Western world that avoid saturated fat.

This is the time to check the preposition of the debate, as we recommended in Chap. 3. In this case the presupposition is that the same diet feet every human being. The fact that there are so many counter examples for each diet might point that this is not the case.

Chapter 7
Metaphysical Disputes

Abstract Metaphysical opinions under dispute often entail strange conclusions. Noticing these conclusions may be interesting, yet they need not be valid counter-arguments; they may, however, suggest to advocates of the metaphysical opinions under dispute to reconsider their views. Some views, mainly metaphysical, refer to claims about future events (for example: one day, it will be possible to construct conscious machines). In debates on such predictions, the contending parties are supposed to show that such events in principle cannot happen or alternately that they should happen as no principle prevents their occurrence. Avoid arguments about whether some entity exists, unless you can agree in advance regarding manageable criteria for admitting or denying its existence. Indeed, such criteria may be subject to preliminary debates.

In what follows, we shall apply the ideas that we have presented thus far to several well-known disputes. Our aim is not to resolve these disputes, but rather to use them as examples of pitfalls that as the default option we recommend to avoid whenever possible. We will review the questions and the main arguments presented in these disputes, and will examine them with an eye to those ideas.

We start with three well-known disputes in the field of Metaphysics. The disputes in this field illustrate three points:

1. No general agreement exists as to the particular question under dispute;
2. Some of the questions that have been under dispute have ceased to catch the interest of knowledgeable parties;
3. Confusion emerges from the fact that several disputants present theories as universal statements while others present them as existential statements.

Before we delve into examples, we should note that the confusions we are discussing are easy to overcome, leading to the disputes being sharpened, not diminished, and thereby made less frustrating. Of disputes that fully diminish or that dissolve, namely that leave no disagreement behind, we say that there were not disputes in the first place, that they only seemed disputes. Wittgenstein-style philosophers find it very satisfactory, and the end of the exercise, the understanding that there was no dispute in the first place. We, on the contrary, follow Kant and Popper in considering this a challenge to rescue the dispute by restating it in a better way or by replacing it with a better one on the same line of concern. We do not deny, however, that Wittgenstein-style philosophers are at times right. Even then we disagree with Wittgenstein's disciples and say, a dispute may dissolve because a presupposition that was the cause of it disappeared; this means that the dispute did exist and that it disappeared only with its presuppositions. That seems to us eminently reasonable, and preferable to Wittgenstein's exposure of metaphysicians as impostors.

All this does not obliterate the fact that, regrettably, on occasion Wittgenstein's disciples are right and the dispute rested on sheer confusion. If so, then, contrary to Wittgenstein and his followers, occasionally vagueness is preferable to clarity, since the study of history requires understanding thing as vaguely or ambiguously as once they were understood. As our example here we take a vague or ambiguous assertion that is unclear about whether it is meant to all or to some of the items it describes: we may speak about a given subject S vaguely or ambiguously, leaving it unclear whether we mean all or only some S. As vague or as ambiguous, then, "people are stupid" may mean, some people are stupid, and it may mean, all people are. This example is not good, as the former statement is obviously true and the latter is obviously false, whereas the significant vague or ambiguous cases are those in which their students were not clear in their minds or unable to decide about the precise meaning of what they were saying.

(This is the greatest folly of Wittgenstein. He claimed that everything that can be said can be said clearly. This is an understandable exaggeration, since originators of important new ideas often learn to say them clearly only after some time, by which time new important ideas are said vaguely or ambiguously. And this process is probably endless. And he deduced from his understandable exaggeration an intolerable proscription on vague or ambiguous speech. For, we learn everything by trial and error, including proper speech. And this means that stuttering is essential for proper speech, so that proscribing stuttering is proscribing all speech.)

And to understand that often the poor statement of problems is the inescapable prelude to their suitable statements helps understand quite a few traditional debates that by now are extinct. This will permit us to comprehend history and see the rationality of the repeated restatements of one problem with increased clarity. What we have said thus far will permit right away to offer a very significant example with no need to explain. The problem that David Hume has raised, the problem of induction, is understood for a century now not as he worded it but as Bertrand Russell did in his classic and very influential *Problems of Philosophy* of 1912. Unlike Hume Russell worded it with no reference to causality.

Ambiguity about all or some—about quantifiers—still excites many philosophers. We do not know why, but we have a conjecture. These philosophers speak of the essence; they find it disturbing that although in essence we are rational, in observed fact we are not, or at least many of us are not. To accommodate for this sad fact, these philosophers find it necessary for the description of the essence of humanity to include the explanation of the fact that rationality is not universally practiced. If this reading is true, then we will stay out of this discussion, since all Aristotelian theories of essence are defective, as modern logic has amply shown; and until the rules of what may count as an essence is reasonably well worded, we find debating essence futile. If and when such a presentation would appear, then they will have to undergo critical discussion in which it should be examined in some detail. It is not that we are not sympathetic to such a discussion, but that we want it to run along proper lines. In particular, stupidity is challenging, no doubt. As Bertrand Russell said, (too many) people would rather die than think; indeed, that is what they usually do. He had in mind such cases as the excitement with which volunteers joined the forces in World War I, for example, only to be slaughtered mercilessly and pointlessly. This event and the general phenomenon of stupidity are puzzling, and they are subject to many interesting and enlightening debates, even if we still do not know the cause of voluntary stupidity. Unfortunately, the philosophers who debate assertions like "people are stupid" do not help clarify this issue because of the inbuilt confusion that they refuse to clear. Russell could use the same words without being too vague or too ambiguous because he had rejected the Aristotelian doctrine of essences offhand. All this is thought provoking. It shows that not the rejection of Aristotelian essentialism but the avoidance of excessive vagueness that counts as advantageous. This raises a simple and vital question: how are we to avoid vagueness? This question is annoying because there is no general rule for it. Still worse, if we do have such a criterion, it may be mistaken and then play havoc. Indeed, the already mentioned famous philosopher Ludwig Wittgenstein claimed that he had such a rule, and for a long time his followers suggested that following his rule leads to utter clarity and prevents prolonged debates, especially the perennial metaphysical ones. It took a generation or two for his fans to admit that he had no such criterion, that indeed he relied on commonsense and on the good sense of those able to put things clearly.

In clear dissent form all versions of Wittgenstein's demand, we will demand nothing and make do with some suggestions that look to us sufficiently reasonable. Indeed, we are often puzzled by the need for restating them. Rather than debate then critically, we will now report on three or four specific examples of classical metaphysical disputes that cover much though not all of classical metaphysics and so much of classical philosophy. We leave it to our readers to decide whether our examples are beneficial or not. If you find them somewhat enlightening, we will be satisfied. If not, we hope that you keep your mind open for efforts of others to improve upon our presentation.

The Mind-Body Problem

Our first case study is the mind-body problem. New scholarly studies devoted to it appear regularly and discuss one aspect of it or another. Most of them do so without wording the question. Some attempts at wording the question are easily available, of course. For example, the *Encyclopedia Britannica* presents the problem by the following sentence:

> Mind-body problem: Metaphysical problem of the relationship between mind and body.

And Wikipedia presents a similar statement:

> The mind-body problem in philosophy examines the relationship between mind and matter, and in particular the relationship between consciousness and the brain,

This is no good, since it is not a question. (Notice that we use the words "problem" and "question" as synonyms, unlike in textbooks, where often problems are exercises and not questions.)

Even papers that do pose the mind-body problem as a question, often do so in a manner that is far from helpful. Ignoring the publications that do not present a question, we list here some questions frequently presented in the relevant literature as the mind-body problem.

> What are the relations between the mind and the body?

This question is too vague, since there are infinitely many such relations, and we find most of them not interesting at all.

> Can a valid distinction be made between the mind and the body?

The answer to this question when taken literally is obviously in the affirmative. A distinction can be made between any two things, and all such distinctions are valid according to some standards of validity or another, though most of them are quite useless.

> Can the mental be reduced to the physical (or *vice-versa*)?

Reduction is a technical word. As long as "if-then" statements are enough for reduction, the answer is obviously in the affirmative, and most reductions are silly and quite unenlightening. If by "reduction" one means logically necessary "if-then" statements, however, then the answer is obviously in the negative, and perhaps in principle so, we do not know.

> Are the mind and the body two different substances?

> Since a substance is an entity that exists necessarily and independently of all else, how can the body and the mind interact?

This question has the great merit that it is the traditional question that great thinkers between Descartes (early seventeenth century) and Russell (early twentieth century) pondered about. It has the drawback of being out-of-date since the substance theory is defunct (due to different assaults on it, by Russell and by Einstein.)

Many philosophers discussed during the seventeenth and eighteenth centuries the last questions in our list. They found it interesting for many reasons, good and bad. One reason is that it smuggled religious discussion into a secular literature: the view of the soul as a substance implies that it is indestructible, as every substance is, being by definition independent on anything else. (The traditional idea that everything utterly independent is indestructible sounds very reasonable. In the early twentieth century the integrity of the nucleus of the atom was deemed independent yet it was assumed that some heavy atoms—the radioactive ones—are likely to disintegrate for no reason at all and with no possibility of any outside influence on their stability or instability. And then it turned out that their instability can be enhanced—as in nuclear explosion—yet the idea of spontaneous disintegration

The Mind-Body Problem

remained a part of nuclear physics to date, so that we no longer take it for granted that the independent is indestructible.) The allegation that the soul is a substance, then, was taken to be the same as that the soul is immortal, that the life of the soul continues after the death of the body. Regrettably, the question whether the soul is a substance or not is no longer interesting; today most philosophers are not interested in substances, much less in their necessary existence. Let us ignore all this and review the discussions to see the patterns of the arguments.

Whatever the traditional mind-body question is, let us look at the answers to it to see if they help us word the question better. The traditional answers are these.

Interactionism: The interaction between the mind and body takes place only in a very small place, the pineal gland (René Descartes).

Parallelism: The mind and the body do not interact but rather operate in parallel according to a Godly pre-determined harmony (Gottfried Wilhelm Leibniz).

Dual aspects theory: The mind and the body are not two substances but rather two aspects of one and the same substance (Benedict Spinoza).

Idealism: The mind and the body are not two substances; rather, the body exists in the mind (Bishop George Berkley).

Materialism: The mind and the body are not two substances; rather, the mind is part of the body (Julien Offray de La Mettrie).

Epiphenomenalism: The interaction between the mind and the body is unidirectional: the body causes mental activity, but not *vice-versa*, very much the way the body throws a shadow. The mind is then just an epiphenomenon of the body (Thomas Henry Huxley).

Neutral monism: there is no substance; rather, both the mind and the body are complex structures of sensations (C. D. Broad).

Each of these answers was criticized as implying strange conclusions. And indeed, all of them are strange. Still, this poses a question: which answer makes the world less strange? And considering this to have been the question under dispute, we should judge quite rational the dispute and the leading arguments in it. In particular, let us report: Berkeley was painfully aware of the strangeness of his idealism and he argued like a lion for his view that materialism was even stranger, since it makes matter indestructible contrary to all experience, and since dualism is even stranger, being inconsistent.

To repeat, nowadays this particular dispute in no longer found interesting, since most of those who discuss the mind-body problem interestingly do not assume that the body or the mind is a substance in the sense of entities whose existence is necessary and independent of anything else. And without this assumption, the whole discussion of substances collapse.

So how should we word the mind-body problem? One suggestion is the following question.

How (if at all) can a physical machine with consciousness be constructed?

(The words "if at all" are redundant, since every question about how or about which way anything happens or takes place, has as one optional answer, "in no way at all".)

The question is challenging: those who claim that we are only physical entities should explain the phenomena of consciousness. Obviously, today no one knows how to build such machine. But our staple question holds. Can one argue these days for/against the view that building such a machine is possible/impossible?

The dispute refers to possible future machines. One party claims that such machines will never be built; the other party claims that they might. When arguing about what will be in the future, the arguments should present difficulties that are in principle insurmountable. The first party should present statements that explain why such a machine cannot be built, due to some familiar difficulties, and should explain why these difficulties should be considered insurmountable. The other party should try to refute these statements or render them highly questionable. Now, as far as we know, all the arguments in defense of the claim that such a machine cannot be built in principle are easily open to criticism. And, obviously, there are no arguments *insuring* that such a machine will ever be possible to build. As a result, the dispute about the question of whether a machine with consciousness can ever be built is interminable as far as we know. Those who wish to see it continued have to find ways to keep it interesting—to themselves and to their opponents alike.

When considering the arguments in this dispute, one should check whether those arguments that the contesting parties present are universal or existential statements, as we have discussed in Chap. 2. Let us mention two examples. Associationism is the idea that all cognitive activity is explicable as a series of associations, where two mental objects are associated if they are similar or if they occur in sufficient proximity of time and place. The arguments that the supporters of this idea present comprise lists of examples of cases that are explicable as associations. Opposing such arguments are usually members of the Würzburg and the Gestalt schools of psychology, who present examples of cases that—they say—are not explicable this way. These arguments presented by the Würzburg and the Gestalt representatives propound an existential statement. They do not have a full-fledged explanation of known information about the working of our cognitive processors. Rather, they alleged that their examples refute the associationist theory of perception and even any similar theory that offers a (quasi-)mechanical explanation of them.

The second example refers to the well-known Chinese room argument. Like the Gestalt's argument, the Chinese room argument and its likes offer no explanation of how we think, but rather they present a thought experiment, alleging that it refutes the theory according to which thinking can be explained as the operation of a computer program. (On the technical sphere, unlike people, computers have no understanding because their operations are all extensional: they have no aims and no preferences although they can be given sets of options with degrees of preferability and then they can behave in a manner that for a while deceives even good experts.)

Our expectations from the arguments presented by rival parties are different. Consider those who present associationism or any other theory that presents mental activity as one that emulates closely a computer-software guided conduct. The rules of the debate may require of them to present arguments showing how such theories explain all the phenomena in question. This they cannot do, and so they may reasonably ask for time out. Those who criticize the theory in question are expected to offer refuting observations, namely, they should present proof of the inconsistency between their observations and the theories that they claim to refute. Hence, it seems that nowadays almost no dispute exists concerning the mind-body problem in the new wording adopted here, since no one has yet succeeded in building a machine that has consciousness or that at least has offered interesting arguments for the claim that such a machine can be built but for some irrelevant limitations (such as limited budgets); nor has anyone presented proof that such a machine *cannot* be built.

Of course, you may claim that our translation of the mind-body problem to a similar problem is objectionable. You may then try your hand—we greatly recommend this—in translating it differently. Even if you fail, we suggest that the exercise may be worth your while. Alternatively, you may open a discussion about the requirements from a translation of a defunct problem. This is a tough assignment, so do not let it frustrate you: true to our system, we recommend that you stop before you get frustrated.

The Problem of Free Choice

We now turn to another classical dispute—about the so-called problem of free choice. In a nutshell, the problem of free choice is as follows: consider any ordinary action, such as raising one's hand. This occurs in the physical world, and as such it is supposed to be determined by natural laws, like any other physical event. Nevertheless, I have a clear sense of being free to choose whether or not to raise my hand, in which case physical laws do not control my choice. The problem of free choice is: what is the proper resolution of is this dilemma or apparent paradox?

Many philosophers have compounded the problem with the dispute between determinism and indeterminism. In a nutshell, this dispute runs as follows: the determinist says that every event that happens in the physical world is predetermined, while the indeterminist claims the opposite, that at least some events in the physical world are not predetermined. It is commonly held, for example, that Newtonian physics is deterministic, while quantum mechanics is not. Furthermore, and still according to received opinion, though not unanimously held, determinism precludes free choice, while indeterminism allows for it. Each of these items is questionable and indeed under dispute. Consider, however, the following obvious argument. To say that a certain event is not predetermined is to say that it is accidental; to say that a certain event is chosen freely is not to say that the choice is accidental or capricious. Hence, whereas determinism (allegedly) precludes free choice, indeterminism offers no explanation for free choice, or even for our mere sense of free choice. Very importantly, there is no theory as to how free choice fits in with physics—this regardless of whether in physics current theory is deterministic or not.

As there may be different reasons for advocating determinism, there are diverse versions of it. The version most popular these days is called scientific determinism, which is a misleading name, since scientific determinism is not scientific but metaphysical. It rests on the understanding that Newtonian mechanics presents a determinist worldview, an understanding that Laplace strongly advocated, so that at times it is called Laplace's determinism. It is inherently deferent from that of the twelfth century philosopher Maimonides that rests on his view that God is omniscient: since He knows the future, it is predetermined. Maimonides was an indeterminist, but he found the determinist argument from God's omniscience disturbingly unanswerable. He found it disturbing, incidentally, since it seems to conflict with the theory of personal providence, namely, the theory of divine rewords and punishments to individuals after their death for their right deeds and for their wrong deeds. Those who do not worry about this as they consider the rewards and punishments in afterlife the results of nothing but God's will are called fatalists.

Note that the problem is neither whether or not we have free will (almost everybody agrees that we have), nor whether or not our conduct is governed by physics (again, almost everybody agrees that it is). The problem rests on the fact that these two ideas seem to clash. Since a clash between accepted ideas is intolerable, we must wonder whether it is real, and if so, what its right resolution is. Notice also, that rationalists do not appeal to providence and perhaps they even deny it, and that the determinism that they may discuss is Laplacean or scientific determinism. To repeat, no one claims for determinism scientific status; rather, it is the affirmative answer to the question, does the latest advanced versions of science claim that the laws of nature fully determine our bodily movements?

When considering a paradox, such as the one that free choice presents, where two statements seem to be both true and yet inconsistent with each other, the options are that either one (or both) of the statements that seem to be true is false, or that the two are consistent with each other. Contrary to what many arguments present in the literature, it is inappropriate to argue that our physics is refuted since we have free will, and it is equally inappropriate to argue that we do not possess free will since (let us agree for the sake of the argument) physics does not allow for it. We have to find a solution that rests on different arguments, showing some deep fault in our way of thinking. Such a solution will enable a better understanding of the world, or, to put it differently, it will decrease the strangeness of the world.

This is the place to mention the philosophy of the influential philosopher Benedict Spinoza. He advocated both scientific determinism and the doctrine of free will. He said, if a stone could think it would think that it wishes to fall in a parabola (the course that Galileo's law of gravity imposes on a falling stone). This may be true or not; not enough is known about either determinism or free will to decide. Participants in this dispute are invited to say more about either or both of these ideas.

We may go further. Suppose determinism is true. Then, as Laplace claimed, a thinker with sufficient information and sufficient calculation power—it is called Laplace's demon—will be able to describe the movements of any object, including the human body, with no reference to any theory but physics. Hence, let us conclude, the demon could calculate the movement of the quilt of a Mozart on a page and thus describe a written piece of music with no knowledge of what music is. This, said the famous quantum physicist, is a pre-established harmony that is hard to conceive. In technical terms this kind of event is said to be over-determined: the written page of music notes follows two sets of rules, those of physics and those of music, where the rules of physics should suffice.

Notice that this is no solution to the problem. It only is the claim that it is hard to believe the idea of Spinoza that the motions of the quilt of a Mozart is determined both by the laws of physics and by the rules of music and the aesthetic sense of the renown composer.

What Is Really the Case?

The mind body problem illustrates a pitfall that is very easily found in many other cases. That we have minds or souls is as obvious as that we are alive: to say that we have souls is to say that we are alive, and living flesh has properties that dead meat does not. Some people object, and wish to distinguish between mind and soul and between having one and being alive. So let us take an adjacent problem that dodged this troublesome move. Consider the question, are we or are humans good or bad? Of course, we know the answer: both. Some of our actions are good, some bad, some of us are good people, some bad. This is not contested. Yet the question is debated for ages. Now whenever a dispute goes on about a question that has undisputed answers, we may suspect that the question is not properly worded. Many people are very happy to destroy a question in hope that it destroys a disagreement. At times they destroy the claim that the two parties debate the same question or the same answer. This is called talking at cross-purposes. All this, we have argued repeatedly, is done in effort to avoid frustrating debates without notice that this kind of move easily increases frustration, since disagreements do not go away when debate about them is suppressed or postponed.

The question, are we good or bad is easily remedied: are we really good or really bad? Some new-age people replace the expression "really" with the word "on the astral plane". Both expressions indicate that the known refutations of the views under debate do not count. Leaving the astral plane aside, let us look at "really". The opposite of the real is the accidental or the apparent, as you wish. The idea is that although our conduct happens to be good or that it happens to be bad, we all have characters, and these reveal themselves only in moment of crisis, whatever these are. The word "character" refers to the theory that each of us, though changeable, has an unchangeable core, and that the core of a person is the real person. This theory is a challenge to find both what characters are possible and what character this or that neighbor of ours has. Thus, the application of the theory of intelligence quotient, of IQ, comes to tell us not what our intelligence is, as this is changeable, say by education, but what is our inborn, unchangeable IQ. There is no such thing, but this does not stop experts apply the theory that it exists and has some characteristic or another. The intelligence quotient does not change; the theory of it does, repeatedly.

We suggest that you avoid discussing what things really are; it suffices that we want to find what they are, and the best way to do so is to ask questions about them, seek answers for these questions, and try to argue about them. It is only when people refuse to lose debates that they move from the search for knowledge about things to the search of real knowledge about them. If they are well trained, they start the debate under conditions that they know make it impossible for them to lose it. Their signal is the question, what is your definition of this, that or the other. What is your definition of life, of the soul, of goodness? Do not argue with these people. The answers they seek are metaphysical and of the kind that blocks all criticism. Respect their wish not to lose a debate, and do not engage in debate with them.

Does God Exist?

Our final example for a metaphysical dispute refers to the existence of God. Any discussion of existence in general is very difficult to manage. Is there a golden mountain (somewhere in the vast universe)? Finding a golden mountain leads to the view that it does exist; otherwise, efforts to find out empirically whether it exists or not are frustrating: one cannot search for it everywhere in order to find out; moreover, we scarcely know where to begin such a search. More generally, whereas existential statements may at times be supported by observations, by themselves they are not undermined by any amount of failures to support them. This is not always the case when the existential statement comes with a full-blown scientific theory. The paradigm case here is that of the rare metal Hafnium. The existence of something like it was predicted already by Dmitri Mendeleevin 1869, as a part of his table of chemical elements, but only when it was repeated as a part of the table of elements of Niels Bohr it became possible to test Bohr's theory by searching for in beds of other rare metals.

Prospectors do seek golden mountains or gold deposits or some other natural resources, be they gold or black gold or any other valuable deposits. Can we not seek out God that way? Let us see how these prospectors seek treasures and see if their techniques work also for the search of God. How then do prospectors go about their business?

Notoriously, different kinds of treasure invite different methods of prospecting; even different prospectors for the same treasure may look for it in different ways. This means that they have some idea as to their probable locations. In particular, they have scientific theories to guide them. But when these suffice, they leave no room for prospecting. And then prospectors leave the scene and applied scientists or engineers replace them. Hence, although prospectors do use scientific theories, they must supplement them with clues, not to mention sheer inarticulate hunches. These are shifty and unreliable, but still they are possibly helpful; alternatively, successful prospectors owe it to sheer luck that they see some success in their prospecting. In this case, prospecting is just a form of gambling, and a wild form at that, since in their case there is no way to calculate the odds. Even when clues and hunches do improve the chances of intelligent prospectors as they guide them in taking their chances, they always take into account the possibility of ending their searches empty-handed. (Otherwise, to repeat, their actions are not that of prospectors but of applied scientists.) Thus, intelligent prospectors are neither fully guided by theory nor blind nor given to sheer luck; usually, they have a reasonably good idea about what a find is, and where it is more likely to find it. (In particular, intelligent prospectors are critically-minded. They tell many stories about mistaken claims for success, and these are warning signs for beginners about kinds of mistakes to avoid.) High-risk investors who invest in gold mining may doubt that specific prospectors have good guidance for their search, and so they may reject the plans of some prospectors, but they also listen to other prospectors and then debate matters with them. If prospectors look for golden mountains, then their debates with possible financial backers about it are better if they follow simple commonsense rules. They should then specify how big a lump of gold must be in order to count as a golden mountain, how pure it must be, and so on. Also, they should explain why the likelihood of encountering a golden mountain is greater in one territory than in another and why they think their clues are promising, as well as what will happen if they do or if they do not find the sought-after treasures. Indeed, before undertaking a debate on the question, "does a golden mountain exist?" it is wise to clarify sufficiently the very ideas of existence and what comprises a golden mountain, so that failure to find one should not lead to a new dispute as to whether what was found does or does not meet our expectations. In other words, although a good debate leads its participants wherever its arguments lead them in an open minded and not pre-determined manner, it is advisable to have a pretty clear initial idea regarding what is the item on the agenda and what proof will be deemed proper termination of the debate.

This advice is dangerous. People who hate to decide can always ask for clarification. Since utter clarity does not exist. (This is the major contribution of Ludwig Wittgenstein: he developed an idea of utter clarity and demanded that it be followed, thus provoking people, such as Bertrand Russell and Kurt Gödel, to disprove this idea.) This raises the question, how clear should we be? What degree of clarity should we aspire to? Karl Popper had a brilliantly simple answer: be sufficiently clear to be able to entertain criticism. This advice is general. Its application may be erroneous. This is why we suggested that discussants should be always ready to stop a debate and move to a meta-debate for a while. This advice is amply illustrated in Plato's early dialogues that are tremendous fun to read as manuals for the conduct of fruitful dialogues. This advice too may be misused: one who wishes to sabotage a debate, you may remember, may constantly demand to shift it, to other debates or to a meta-debate. A foolproof manual cannot exist. This should suffice as a preliminary to our discussion of discussions of the existence of God.

We have tried to dodge this traditional discussion. Noticing that prospectors seek gold without knowing whether our surrogate question is this. Is it possible to seek the Creator the way prospectors seek gold—not knowing whether He exists? Perhaps. First let us ask how far the parallel between theology and prospecting can go. When a golden mountain is found, we may decide that it exists and avoid further discussion of the matter. For this, you remember, we have to specify in advance what qualifies as a golden mountain. Do such specifications exist for the conceivable success in the search for the Creator? This question is unavoidable if frustration is to be avoided. And so we would like to dwell on it, yet it is a very difficult question. How then should we go about it? We do not know. But let us try, very tentatively. To consider the question of the existence of the Creator as akin to the question of the existence of a golden mountain, then, we suggest, one should first inquire regarding what theory and which clues may lead the search and improve the odds of a successful outcome, not to mention the decision as to claims that we have found Him. Existent theories are thus far all worthless, as it is not clear to us as yet to what kind of Creator the discussion concerns, let alone claims to have found Him. We may try to decide on this by looking at received traditions. As it happens, two Western traditions concern two characterizations of the Creators: the one described in the western monotheistic or Abrahamic religions (Jewish, Christian, or Muslim) as described in their relative scriptures and the other that philosophers—ancient and modern alike—discuss with no reference to any sacred text. The two kinds of theories, or rather the religions that they represent, philosophers call by different names: the revealed (where the revelation is described in given Scriptures) and the natural (or universal or rational). As Heinrich Heine has already complained (*Religion and Philosophy in Germany: A Fragment*, 1834), these two kind of theories (or of religions) are confused regularly and systematically. As to clues, one big clue exists, traditionally known by the name that Robert Boyle (of Boyle's law) gave it: the physico-theological argument for the existence of God. Later on it was rechristened by other names, the latest being, the argument from intelligent design: the world is a marvelous clock; hence, there should be a designer and maker of this clock. This notion has raised much discussion about the question, how marvelous this clockwork is, given global injustice. (There are many examples for this. Ivan Karamazov discussed the case of a parent who mistakenly punishing an innocent child; today the staple examples are Auschwitz and/or Hiroshima). Neo-Darwinians use examples from allegedly faulty design of animals, since Darwinism stresses that the fittest survives even though they are not quite fit. Quite generally, the argument from design raises the question, how really intelligent is the intelligent design when Nature shows so many seeming defects? This question is often dismissed by the observation that the beauty of the world of ours is breathtaking regardless of all its faults. This observation is eminently true but quite irrelevant. For, the Creator is described as perfect, and this world of ours, wonderful and admirable and delightful as it may be despite its faults is faulty nonetheless, and so it does not quite become the Creator if He is almighty. The answer to this most obviously valid and reasonable objection is that the Creator is impeccable but as He gave us free will we have used our freedom and created evil. This introduction of free will raises more difficulties than it resolves, of course; moreover, there is enough evil for the objection to hold that has nothing to do with human interference. To this the defender of the argument from design say, the ways of the Lord are mysterious. This is most likely to be true. So it sounds as if it is a reasonable answer to the latest version of the objection to the argument from intelligent design. It is not. Indeed, it is a declaration of bankruptcy. For, had the defenders of the view that the Creator exists began the discussion by admitting that His ways are mysterious, we would not take recourse to the argument from design in the first place. We asked, what can we say about the Creator, so that when we encounter Him we will agree that He does exist indeed.

The preliminary discussion as we have developed it here in order to avoid frustration has thus become extremely frustrating. We suggest that this is so because a clue with no theory cannot lead to a simple assessment that should be initially agreed upon (if frustration is to be avoided). So we do not know under what conditions which party should concede defeat, the party that speaks for the existence of the alleged Maker of the clockwork that our wonderful universe is or the party that denies this existence. If we cannot agree about the way to identify the Creator's handiworks, we cannot identify the Creator either, even if He will reveal Himself to us on Mount Sinai or on Mount of Olives or in Mecca (or elsewhere). This amounts to the assurance that the dispute will frustrate its participants.

Can we then prepare the debate about the question of the existence of the Creator by seeking a theory about Him? This is doubtful. The great mediaeval theologian Moses Maimonides declared it impossible to know what attributes if any become the Lord; indeed, he said, human language is too poor for that. How then can we prepare for such a debate so as to avoid frustration? We propose to take a step backward and ask, why does this interest us and what does it matter? We mean this not as rhetoric question, of course, and not as a mere preliminary, but as a debate-stopper. (Indeed, we have asserted repeatedly, we find most of the debates that take place quite pointless, so that the discussion of the question, why do they matter, would have prevented them and thus saved much frustration and waste of energy.) Not in the present case, though: in the present case it is very easy to answer the question. Whether God exists or not is indeed the most important question we could possibly ask, since if He does exist, then worshiping Him is clearly the most valuable task. But this answer is not trouble-free. Suppose that He does exist, what then is the proper worship of Him? The default answer is, proper conduct: the right way to worship Him is by behaving properly. This answer is too good, as proper behavior is imperative regardless of the answer to the question at hand. What conduct then is the proper worship of Him if and only if the Lord does exist? For example, is it proper to sacrifice animals for his greater glory? In ancient times Jews said, yes, of course. Maimonides said, of course not: it is an insult to the Great God. We cannot know unless we know something about Him. True, traditional religion tells us. Modern philosophers—including some who were very religious—rejected the traditional answer offhand, before hearing it, on the ground that traditional religion has no authority over us. It imposes itself on us rationally or unjustly. If rationally, then we do not need it as we should use reason; if unjustly, then it robs us of our freedom of thought. Those philosophers, who were religious despite their refusal to accept that authority of religion, claimed that reason directs us to the endorsement of traditional religion. This, to repeat, other philosophers find doubtful. They may also find it harmful, as reason unifies humanity yet religion splits it. Still, some philosophers, notably Martin Buber, said that accepting traditional religion in the name of reason cleans it of its rationally unacceptable parts, while offering the religion we were born into as our own default option, or even the only option available. This does not solve the problem: we should know when it makes sense to accept our religious tradition and when it does not; hence, what is the default option is not the issue, and we have no idea which religion to follow—yours or mine. No matter what your answer to this question is, you must consider it. Hence, you have to consider some idea, be it originally a part of your traditional religion or any traditional religion or a religion that is not traditional at all.

Of courses, some people—perhaps most people—will disagree and say that some traditional ideas, especially some traditional religious ideas, are obligatory to endorse and are not up for negotiation. Yet, although many people would agree with this, few of them mean it literally. It may be wiser to avoid debate with such people: they may wish to convince you of the validity of their own religion, but they refuse to put theirs in question, which is legitimate, of course; so is the refusal to argue with them that we recommend on the basis of our view that lacking reciprocal willingness to accept criticism, debate is useless. So, if you must argue with them, perhaps you will do well to insist on speaking with them only about what they and you are in agreement about. Those who say that traditional religion is obligatory and do not quite mean what they say, they often know that they exaggerate. They know that no ancient religion will be fully endorsed today by any reasonable person, and even they will reject at least some ancient traditional religious ideas. They may take this in their stride, considering the religious ideas that they reject marginal and not intended to take literally. Indeed, all religions require some reconsideration or reinterpretation in the light of new knowledge. And so we are back at the need to weigh ideas, even traditional religious ideas. Which brings us back to the critical attitude to religion that most philosophers adopt, no matter how sympathetic to religion they may be or how religiously committed they are.

This in turn brings us back to the Creator as philosophers have conceived Him, not the Creator of traditional religion. What is known about Him? After the Middle Ages traditional philosophy defined the divinity as perfection itself. We know now that Maimonides was right: we do not know what perfection is; we can scarcely imagine it without getting into paradoxes. What else then is known about Him? Nothing.

This, we say, is where our discussion should better stop. We advise you then to decline the invitation of those who want to follow it further. Otherwise, we advise you to condition the acceptance of the invitation to continue the discussion on the ability of your interlocutors to explain a bit better the question they wish to discuss further with you. The latest effort in this direction, to repeat, is the famous idea of intelligent design. The advantage of this idea is that it expresses no bias in favor of any specific religion, or, more precisely, that it suppresses such expressions as a kind of temporary accord between leaders of different American churches to overlook their differences while struggling in courts with those who want them to keep out of politics (more specifically, to keep prayers out of state schools) as the constitutional separation of church and sates requires. The disadvantage of our advice is that we despair of efforts to understand the traditional idea of the Creator (religious and philosophical alike). Efforts to understand this idea (or its parallels in Oriental thought) will continue, and if someone will be able to meet our challenge better than we can see, then the debate may reopen with little or no frustration. All this lies well beyond the scope of this handbook.

Chapter 8
Disputes About History and Predictions

Abstract Debates on certain historical narratives may suggest looking for predictions implied by the hypothesis that they are (or are not) true and then to test these predictions by studying more detailed texts or even historical records. It might also be advisable to check whether the events narrated could be expected under common general assumptions regarding human behavior. The same holds regarding some long-range predictions. In debates about subjunctive conditional statements (answers to questions of the form "what would have happened if …?" of the form "if x were the case than y would be too"), it is advisable to consider the degree to which one event usually serves as means for predicting the other. This advice resembles the above-mentioned one about causality.

The above discussion of some major metaphysical issues came to illustrate our suggestion that discussions of existential statements are frustrating and so they are better avoided when possible. (Note: not all metaphysical assertions or theories are existential. Indeed, the report of Aristotle on the ancient metaphysics in his famous history of metaphysics that is the opening of his book on the subject mentions only universal theories. The first, of Thales, "All is water", is still the paradigm case. The assertion that God exists did not interest Aristotle; his discussions of existence systematically referred to observed phenomena, such as change, and their causes and their effects; this seemed to him sufficient reason to refer to God as the perfect being that will not change, the unmoved mover. This is his version of the philosophical divinity.)

There is a limit, of course, to the possibility to follow our advice to avoid discussions of existential statements and our suggestion is that if you do discuss them, try first to put them as much in context as possible. Our advice rests on the fact that the introduction of existential statements into a theoretical debate either plays a significant role as refutations of universal statements, which is at the heart of all critical debate, or else they are often introduced into theoretical debates as theories, and then they are highly frustrating, and thus items that we advise our readers to avoid whenever possible in effort to reduce their frustration, or at least describe their context first. This will help, since discussing the reason why an existential theory is introduced helps contrive a context to it that may help see the point of the discussion and then at least we can see if the point was reached or missed. Our example, from the existence of God, comes because we admit that the question may be very important, and we have tried to see whether the debate does hope reach or come close to the aim of the discussion that this aim prescribes. Some readers may find this example unsatisfactory since theology always has a special place in our tradition, for good or ill. So let us take another example of discussions of existential statements, and one that is scarcely avoidable: history; any history, especially political or social.

The limit to our advice to avoid discussions of existential theories is in historical discussions, since all history deals exclusively with existential statements. This sounds false, as there is also hypothetical history subjunctive-conditional or hypothetical or conjectural history, at times called the history of the what if. For, contrary to severe reprimands, this history does exist. And we do not object it: we think it is all to the good, as those who proscribe it need not read it. (They do.) Even this kind of history, we contend, is all existential. It opens with descriptions of some past facts, including events that did happen due to chance or to some choice, on the hypothesis that some accidents or some choices or other could happen differently, and assuming for the sake of their discussion that these happened differently. In discussions of hypothetical history, a question arises, what would have been the course of history had it developed on a different possible line. These teach us in depth about the accidents and the choices that (we all agree) did take place in the past. An example will make this easier to perceive. Dramatist Carl Zuckmayer said, had the Nazis won the War their regime would have collapsed as it was hopelessly corrupt. This is the observation about the existence of corruption in that regime, the assertion that it was a part of the ideology of that regime, and the unproblematic theory (the theory that all participants in the discussion endorse) that there is a limit to the corruption that a successful regime can tolerate. Whether the observation of Zuckmayer is true or false is not our concern in the present paragraph (we will take this up soon enough); rather, here it is an example of our contention that historians too make and discuss existential statements. Zuckmayer did observe something about the Nazi regime that was not sufficiently noted by others: it was corrupt intolerably, and its corruption was due to its violent ideology.

This example is terrific. And so we have to issue a warning: examples may be seductive; indeed, good examples are. And so it is important to say, especially in a handbook for rational debates, against everything seductive: when you are open to seduction, you are better off knowing this. And you are always better off knowing that a seductive instance is no substitute for a rational argument. A good example for a theory may be presented artistically in a powerful narrative, and it is then to be enjoyed, but as propaganda not as arguments. (Not all propaganda is objectionable, but even propaganda for a good cause is objectionable if it is an argument-surrogate.) Often, books that advocate outlandish ideas comprise series of examples. They do the job of making their theses seem less strange in the sense that they help their readers get used to them, but they do not even make them less strange in the sense that we have used this word in this handbook, let alone making them rationally appealing. And so we do not intend to use our example from conjectural history as convincing, since all conjectural history is strange, and we want to discuss a bit more critically our contention that all history is a series of existential assertions and rational—critical—discussions about them. Intuitively, then, we have now a few options as to what aspect of history to discuss next. Several types of disputes have emerged regarding history, and naturally we may now take up any one of them. They are as follows.

1. Disputes about historical *facts*: what exactly happened in a certain place and time, or, is the report about a certain historical event true. For example, did Socrates exist or is he the invention of Plato?
2. Disputes about historical *causes*: what were the causes for a certain historical event? For example, why was Socrates sentenced to death? More interestingly, what are the causes for the First World War? What led to it?
3. Disputes about historical *subjunctive conditionals or hypotheticals* (of the kind that the example we have just offered): what would have happened if a certain historical event had occurred or had not occurred? For example, what would have happened had the USA dropped nuclear bombs on the Second World War on Mount Fuji rather than on Hiroshima and Nagasaki (as some of the scientists involved say they had preferred)?

Before delving into these questions, we may find it helpful to consider why some questions about history are interesting in the first place. For, to repeat, an answer to this question may guide us in our effort to reduce frustration in debates. We may also ask, why do many historians proscribe debating hypothetical historical questions, and are they right?

Let us start then with the most basic question: why are some questions about history interesting? One popular answer to this question is that history can teach us some practical lessons. Some historical cases are similar to present cases, and they may help us avoid repeating historical mistakes. Here is a famous example. In 2008, economists in the USA said that the financial crisis of that time resembled that of 1929, and they recommended avoiding the mistakes that rendered the consequences of the 1929 crisis so abysmal. Such a conclusion is easily contested: we do not know what mistakes aggravated the situation then. Instead, we can learn from history by *finding cases that refute ideas*. Consider, for example, the most popular argument in favor of keeping illegal the use of mind-affecting drugs, according to which decriminalizing the use of these drugs will render drug use excessively popular and thus risk the very ability to maintain civil society. The idea behind this argument is that the availability of drugs and the freedom to use them renders their use excessive. This idea is refuted by historical evidence from the availability of drugs and the freedom to use them, say, in nineteenth-century China (and, indeed, in all countries prior to the twentieth century). Moreover, it is possible to learn from the failure of the more recent prohibition in the USA to reduce the consumption of alcohol and choose to abolish similar current prohibitions. This argument need not be devastating, and indeed the debate goes on; our point is that it is valuable because this argument may be useful to some extent.

This is not the complete answer to our question: the study of history is useful for additional reasons. We need not go into them, as we are interested in history even when we do not learn any practical lesson from it. Indeed, another reason for learning about history is our wish to understand our current situation from a broader perspective than we already have: the wish to broaden our perspectives on current affairs invites the study of history in the hope that history will somehow help us understand the current situation by telling us how things have come to be as they are. The events recorded by historians, then, are supposed to throw light on the present state of affairs. In other words, by studying history, we hope to reveal the processes that brought about the present situation and that understanding these processes will make the present state of affair less surprising or less unexpected. This is true for all the fields of study: the history of economics, technology, or science can help us understand the current situation within economics, technology, or science. There are special aspects to special kinds of history. Thus, the history of mediaeval music teaches us differently than recent political history; moreover, the worst errors in the history of mediaeval music have a different status from the worst error in recent political history. The latter are a part of our heritage and we have to do more to correct them than we have to do to correct mistakes in the history of mediaeval music, where at times publishing a correction in a learned periodical will do. Similarly, errors about the role of political history in the life of the nation are unfortunately not easily corrected.

Thus, teachers of political history often ignore the best explanations for the interest in history. School history *curricula* pay much attention to ancient and mediaeval history, advancing slowly to modern times, usually failing to reach the present—thereby failing to point at the relevance of historical events to the present. Not surprisingly, then, many students find history dull and uninteresting. History teachers may inspire interest by considering the following half-baked idea: start with a very quick review of human history, and then review the historical events backward, starting with events relevant to current affairs, and then moving to the still older events that explains the old events, and so on into the mist of our distant past.

Back to the questions raised in the opening of this chapter. When debating whether or not a certain historical assertions are true, obviously we cannot resolve the dispute by direct observation, since the alleged event was in the past. However, we can still try to find facts that are implied by the alleged event and can be observed today. For example, archeologists may dig into battlefields and check the devastation that battles allegedly have caused. Suppose our interest is in considering events whose legal registry the law requires. One may consult record books to check whether these events are recorded as was required. Suppose such records are not found where they should be present. This need not disprove the claim that the event took place, as it is possible to try and explain why the event has evaded recording in light of how the law in question was understood at the time. (If the explanation of the absence of a record refers to some unspecified conspiracy, though, then it is worthless—as we have already explained.) Suppose the case is still more problematic: suppose someone suggests a new theory about the assassination of President Kennedy. It makes sense to try to find some non-trivial implications of the suggested theory that can still be observed. If the theory relates to the number of bullets that hit the President, then we may try to check the available photos, the autopsy report, etc. As was mentioned in Chap. 4, there is big difference between predicting something that we do not know yet and explaining an already known fact. This example becomes interesting if a predicted item of evidence to be found in records is new, or if it evaded earlier inspections because no one had paid attention to it as it was not considered interesting. The basic principle is the one mentioned in Chap. 4: a theory (about a historical occurrence) is interesting if it makes the world less strange. President Kennedy's assassination is quite strange given the tremendous apparatus of his bodyguards, and perhaps this is the reason why so many theories have been suggested about it. We leave it to our readers to decide whether one of these theories succeeds in making this event less strange. We might add here, perhaps, that historians committed to the conspiracy theory tend to see history, perhaps the whole social world, as very strange, like movies of Oliver Stone, especially his 1991 movie JFK about the assassination. This is not specific to conspiracy narratives. Consider the books by the sociologist Erving Goffman that are mainly series of very interesting case studies. The supposition that all everyday social events are as strange as the ones he describes render the world very strange. What we can learn from the events he describes, incidentally, is that many common ideas that are deemed commonsense and so obviously true are not true.

Let us move, then, to a more intricate matter, to our second question. It concerns disputes about the historical causes. Causal questions are more difficult to handle than the questions of mere occurrences, and as mentioned in Chap. 5, we have recommended avoiding discussion causality when possible. The analogy from natural science suggests that an explanation should have the structure of a logical argument implying the event to be explained from a theory (putatively considered true) and some known facts. Admittedly, this model has been under a long dispute among philosophers of history. Some of them claimed that there are no non-trivial generalizations that hold throughout history, and therefore the model that applies in the natural sciences is inapplicable to history. This dispute is insignificant. It is possible to skip it and yet follow the suggestion made here in regard to the search for a theory that makes the world less strange, and even while applying to the case under study only generalizations that we may take as trivial, namely, generalizations not under dispute. (This is not a limitation: when a thinker presents a case history while applying to it a controversial generalization, then the debate about the presentation will include a debate about that generalization, and that debate will not be considered history. Thus, when Sigmund Freud applied his theory of the Oedipus complex to the case of Moses the law giver, the study is deemed more a part of psychoanalytic theory than of history.) Disputes regarding historical causes often include efforts to check how much the explanation under discussion agrees with our expectation in regard to human behavior and ideas. A mistake is lurking here, however: it seems natural to assume that a familiar event plus a familiar theory cannot yield a surprising result. Consider the explanation of the strange fact that in the famous Moscow show trials of leading communists, the accused confessed to crimes that obviously they could not have committed, so that the confessions were acts of self-sacrifice. One possibly reasonable explanation for this is that the accused were trying to cooperate with the regime to the last. Another is that they were promised safety for their loved ones in exchange. We offer these explanations not as true but as *reasonable and possibly true*. They both rest on trivial generalizations: that people dedicated to a cause are prone to sacrifice themselves for it and that people will sacrifice themselves to save their loved ones.

Historical explanations that do not employ trivial generalizations, like the one of Freud just mentioned, are easy to find. All one needs is the application of a controversial theory to history, such as Marxism or psychoanalysis. A number of historical explanation use Freud's theory of the Oedipus complex that we have already mentioned. To repeat, we need not dismiss his explanations because the theory of the Oedipus complex is still quite controversial, as we view it as a part of the discussion as pertaining more to Freud's theory than to history. If and when we will consider that theory trivial, if and when it will be admitted with no question, then we will deem some Freudian explanations historical rather than psychoanalytical. Until then, such explanations are taken more as discussions of those theories than as discussions of history. Thus, nothing hinges on the fact that the generalizations used in historical explanations are or are not trivial. The fact that they are usually trivial is used to explain the strange fact that historians seldom refer to laws (i.e., they do not make generalizations). For example, when they use evidence to support or refute historical explanations, logic requires a link between the explaining and the explained statements of particular events, and the link is either an *ad hoc* hypothesis or a generalization. If the generalization is not stated, says Karl Popper (*The Open Society and Its Enemies*, final chapter), this is because it is too trivial to require explicit assertion. Taking his explanation of the conduct of historians out of context, critics considered it a generalization about historians, although it is but an explanation of an oddity in their conduct, given the theory of explanation. He has thus rendered a phenomenon that looks strange quite commonsense and thus not strange at all.

To repeat, the conduct of historians (who explain with no reference to generalizations) seems at odds with the view of philosophers of history (that every reasonable explanation includes a generalization). This may seem odd (to people who have high opinions on all of them as serious scholars). And then this may be challenging to seek some explanation that will make their conduct less odd. Popper has offered one. There may be other: quite a few candidates propose themselves. We leave this discussion to our readers to complete as an exercise.

We now turn to our third question, and it is even more intricate. It concerns hypothetical history. Clearly, this is a kind of subjunctive conditionals, so-called: were x true then y would hold. Conditional statements (if x then y), with false antecedents (x is false) are always true (vacuously true). Not so subjunctive conditionals: we all agree that whereas the statement "had I jumped from the Empire State Building I would die" differs from "had I jumped from the Empire State Building I would fly" and most of us, if not all of us, will agree that the first is true and the second is false. When discussing subjunctive conditionals we face the problem: how, if at all, are they open to examination? Subjunctive conditionals come in a very great variety. The example that we have just given assumes false statements about situations while taking the laws of nature to hold, or, what would have happened if a certain event would have happened differently from the way it did. (When I stood there I could fall but did not.) An example may concern what would happen if a certain law of nature were slightly different from what it is. Strictly speaking, such a question is awesome. Any event that has happened is the result of events going back to the Big Bang (assuming that this event did take place), and any effort to explain the assumption that it happened differently from the way it did might lead to assumptions of changes along the entire history of the universe; or not—this depends on the extent to which laws of nature have determined the event in question, strict ones or merely statistical. If the latter is the main cause, then perhaps explanation of a subjunctive conditional here on earth should go back only as far as the formation of the solar system or much less. We do not know, and it does not matter at all. For, obviously, this is not what is interesting about discussions of questions such as, what would have happened had the USA not used nuclear weapons in World War Two or had it dropped the bomb not on Hiroshima but on Mount Fuji. Usually we just look for a reasonable possibility: one that concurs with our expectations in regard to human views, values, and conduct. We speak in the subjunctive mode while imagining a reasonably minimal difference between a real and a hypothetical case—assuming we can get to agreement about it. In this sense, our third question resembles the second: discussing whether one event usually follows another is relevant to the question of what would have happened had the causal event not occurred. And so, to prevent frustration in debating subjunctive conditionals, we propose that the parties to the debate prepare it carefully by clarifying to themselves reasonably well both what propels the debate and what kind of subjunctive conditional is on the agenda for debate. Moreover, let us repeat, we contend that standing debates have important core even if they are poorly conducted so that the core is hidden. Hence, when some possible case histories persist, they look significant. As this significance may be unclear, the effects of one answer or an alternative to it may be not easily made apparent. They may be consequences that matter under conditions greatly different from the ones we live in, or they may relate to different places or different times. These matter if, say, the different time is the remote future. Somehow, we care about the future of our great-great children, which may make us care about questions that pertain to our distant future. This leads us to debates about situations that may occur in the near future. Let us glance at such debates.

Long-Range Forecasts

Disputes about long-range forecasts are similar to disputes about history: neither is given to resolution by straightforward observations, although in some cases, some ingenuity may lead to some unexpected and intriguing tests of such theories. These tests will of course comprise some predictions, and these may help resolve the dispute or at least advance it somewhat so that it will not be as utterly frustrating as such disputes tend to be. For example, when disputing about long-term predictions regarding global economy, it makes sense to search for the theory that would yield the prediction under discussion and to check this theory in the same way we check any scientific theory or hypothesis: by appeal to repeatable observations that we can perform here and now with reasonable efforts.

Some scholars have claimed that historical development obeys certain rules and argued that we could uncover these rules and apply them to make scientific predictions regarding future events. They admit that the means for detailed predictions of the distant future of social or political affairs are not available, but the state that great events, like eclipses, are already predictable. These phenomena are called revolutions. An example of an important and predictable revolution is a political revolution like a change of regime. This is the doctrine of historical inevitability that Karl Popper has called historicism and severely criticized as unscientific, as untestable in principle: all known sufficiently precise versions of it were refuted long ago. He repeated the powerful argument of Henri Poincaré: nothing influences the course of history as profoundly as new ideas, and new ideas are inherently unpredictable. (Predicting a future idea makes it present. Of course, there is an obvious answer to this objection: we can predict the future idea in general but not in the details needed to make it present. This answer is valid and therefore historicism is not refutable; only the versions that are sufficiently detailed to be refutable are already refuted.) Other scholars have suggested that we can predict future events by extrapolating current trends. This is another type of historicism, which can have an indefinite number of versions, as there are many variables to extrapolate and (infinitely) many ways to extrapolate every one of them from any given set of data. This is obviously true, unless some theory limits the options to a reasonably small number. We may have some partial theories that explain given trends and try to extrapolate on the basis of observations of these trends. But then there would be no theory to help predict which among various conflicting trends will continue and which will terminate. Karl Marx noted that industrial enterprises grow steadily. This growth had a good rationale: bigger steam-engines are more efficient and bigger concerns may be better organized (compare the supermarket with the traditional local store). So Marx predicted that competition will radically reduce the middle classes (such as store owners). The appearance of the electric dynamo changed all that, however, as it enabled the creation of myriads of small enterprises. And then came aviation and destroyed the trend of building ever bigger boats, yet without creating small aviation enterprises; this may change any day with the advancement of aviation techniques. Is this a refutation of Marx's theory? It is not clear. Marx expected the socialist revolution to take place in the industrial part of the world. Vladimir Lenin disagreed with him. Some people considered Lenin's revolution to be in disaccord with Marx; others said the two might coincide. As long as we do not know what exactly Marx's theory is, this dispute is very frustrating and so it is better avoided. If you must partake in a discussion on this or on a similar matter, you will avoid much frustration by insisting on agreement between participants about *what particular theory is under scrutiny* in that discussion.

This sounds obvious and commonsensical; yet many discussions concern unstated theories, especially in psychology and in economics but also generally in politics. We should explain why. Perhaps the reason is that defining the initial terms is actually not so simple. Other options are obvious; we will not discuss them here.

Can Marx's theory be put to test? To answer this question, we need a definitive version of his theory, the way we have a definite version of Euclidean geometry or of Newtonian mechanics. (Such theories, or their agreed-upon versions, may gain consensus, and then people declare them canonic. The word "canonic" means accepted; the expression "canonic version" stems from the version of a sacred text that is officially recognized as the right one.) These definitive versions were achieved over centuries of great efforts. So perhaps at some future moment, we will have a definitive version of Marx's theory of history, which will then be easier to discuss with little or no frustration. At present, however, we may disagree as to whether the failure of the communist countries developed on the basis of this theory. To repeat our earlier suggestion, if you wish to avoid frustration, do not enter such a debate before the diverse parties agree about the sufficiently precise version of Marx's theory that they wish to debate, or, better still, agree to the question that his theory came to answer and hopefully also the alternative answers to it.

Perhaps we are too categorical. People often behave as if they hope that discussing a doctrine that is not properly and definitely worded may help clarify it and word it satisfactorily. When doing so, then refuting the theory does not count as it is considered a refutation of an initial, tentative wording of it. Only after it was debugged can it be put to a real test. This is a common if seldom articulated idea. It is nonetheless mistaken. It is an attitude that is simultaneously defensive and hyper-critical. Its defensiveness is clear: it is the tendency to view all errors as verbal. Surprisingly, it is still also hyper-critical since it encourages making a correction whenever an error was found: it rests on the false premise that any possible refutation serves as possible evidence for a mistake. Nevertheless, we are willing to endorse such means as a temporary measure, leading to rewording prior to a point when we have a version ready for a critical debate. For, evidently, a debate starts in earnest when a question and its competing answers are on the table. All else is preliminary. To repeat, we greatly recommend good preliminaries as they prevent much frustration. Yet they can be frustrating too, when we are anxious to begin the debate yet some of us who are more cautious than the rest of us insisting on continuing with the preliminaries. In such cases, conduct that may be highly frustrating is taken in good humor in the hope of seeing some progress. As usual, in seeking any progress, like in prospecting, it is good to identify how much patience we have before declaring the venture futile. In general, though, we recommend avoidance of any dispute that rests on historicism, as it is more likely to frustrate than to bear fruit.

Let us draw attention to one ploy that prevents all knowledge to avoid certain kinds of debate, scientific and more so metaphysical: dilute the question. Thus, when we learn that we cannot profit from historicist debates, we can easily dilute them: rather than discuss the historicist question of the future of humanity, we can discuss what is known as global politics. Look at the map of the globe and see it divided into circles of influence. Consider that influences increase by expansions and try to guess the next probable expansion of this or that empire. This sounds exciting but it is rather boring as it is much more arbitrary than it looks at first sight.

Global Famine

We will end this chapter by reviewing the debate about the risk of global famine.

The question under dispute is:

Is the world face a high risk of hunger? If so, what is the best way to decrease this risk?

The question became popular in political discussion following the very famous *An Essay on the Principle of Population* of Thomas Robert Malthus, published at the end of the eighteenth century. He extrapolated the increase of the human population and the potential increase of food: the size of the population increases in geometrical series and the size of food in arithmetical series. Hence, he concluded, the world's population will soon face famine. The only way to prevent this is to apply drastic steps in order to reduce the growth of the population. The most valuable aspect of his theory is his criticism of a very important tacit assumption in classic economic theory, namely, that all natural resources are unlimited although the investment of labor to access them vary. The detail of the theory, namely the growth rate, is of course most inaccurate, just as the assertion about starvation is, since starvation takes place all the time. The most important influence Malthus had was on Darwin's theory of natural selection. For, the idea of Malthus that food grows less rapidly than the human population is questionable: why should all species grow geometrically? Any single plant species, said Darwin, has so many seeds, that unchecked it will cover the whole earth in little time.

The prediction of Malthus about global catastrophe led to the idea of family planning. Human population still continues to grow in great rate, but it is reduced with the rise of standard of living, and food production also grows, largely but not only due to innovations in agriculture. The fear from global famine due to overpopulation is nonetheless still under debate.

There is no way to predict future innovations (if we had a theory that would enable prediction of them, we would test it and possibly apply it now). The most important factor seems to be the rise in the standard of living—including the rise in life expectancy. It seems that all over the world, whenever people can hope that almost all their children will grow up healthy and that having fewer children will allow them to provide improved childcare and improved education, then they voluntarily decrease the number of their offspring. The question remains under debate whether this suffices as means to avert the danger of global instability due to overpopulation.

Chapter 9
Disputes About Technology, Including Medicine

Abstract In disputes about technological, ethical, and political problems, the disputing parties may agree about the list of advantages and disadvantages of each of the possible options that the competing answers offer, yet disagree about the benefits of these advantages and the cost of these disadvantages. Such disputes are usually not theoretical, and then disputants may try to concentrate on evaluating these costs and benefits.

Many disputes refer to technological questions regarding technology in general (or applied science), physical technology, biological or human nature, military affairs, medical issues, the media, and other issues. Here are examples of some types of common technological questions.

1. Should we (i.e., humanity, my country, my firm, my family, myself) adopt a given technology? Example: should governments/the government of my country/medical authorities demand/encourage/allow/prohibit/the use of a given drug/medication?
2. Which technology is best for solving a given problem? Example: which alternative energy source should we (humanity/my country) adopt? Another example: what energy (gas/electricity) is preferable (nationally/personally) for the running of household implements?
3. Which technological problem should we tackle and how? Example: which medical research should the government support as top priority, cancer research or AIDS research? Another example: as any foundation supporting cancer research is flooded with applications for grants to support diverse cancer research projects, how should it decide which of these applications to support? Still another example: should we (my government/my research institute/my car manufacturing company) investigate the possibility of mass-production of cars with engines run not on internal combustion?

Two major differences exist between disputes in technology (and applied science) and disputes in other fields (pure science, basic science, metaphysics, etc.). First, questions in pure science and in metaphysics are interesting as long as they are relevant to the big questions, such as, what does it mean to be human? What does it amount to? How was the world created? Technological questions do not meet this criterion. They are interesting as long as they are relevant for increasing our welfare, even if they contribute nothing to the understanding of the world. Even when technological research concerns a law of nature, the law may signify more practically than intellectually. And then it is called basic research.

The automation of any manufacturing process may serve as an example of a technological problem that has scarcely any intellectual value. A more intriguing example is the effort to create a variant of some medication—say to serve as a cure for some disease—even when we have no understanding of how the initial medication works, let alone its variants. The discovery of aspirin (salicylic acid) and the search for its better substitutes or for its derivatives offer a famous example of a medication whose utility was discovered before any theory was available of the working of its mechanism and those of its early substitutes and derivatives.

The second major difference between disputes in technology and in other fields is this. When asked whether a certain scientific theory is true, one option we have is to suspend judgment, to abstain from providing an answer. If we have no idea whether a theory makes sense or not, we can simply say so. In the abstract, cautious abstention from taking a position regarding the truth or falsity of a theory need not incur any penalty. Often researchers express assent to a theory that has just won the consensus even if they have not yet studied it in depth, and this is but another way to suspend judgment for a while. This is particularly true of societies where the opposite is not true, where asserting the wrong answer may lead to public shaming and even loss of income. This is not the case, however, when considering technology, for example, the use of a new, potentially effective medication: as long as it is not explicitly approved of, it is forbidden, and then those who could use it might suffer needlessly. This is not true of researchers: they have to follow a promising lead and may even be charged of neglect if they do not. Indeed, researchers may prefer to apply refuted theories, since their refutations make it clear what are the limits of their applicability. This is also true for the generals whose task is to equip their armies with the up-to-date most efficient weapons.

We have to apply here a somewhat formal terminology, but this is hardly problematic. Discussions about the advisability of the adoption of a given technology involve two types of errors: false negative and false positive. False negative is the error of preventing the use of an efficient means (say, medication; the error is in the adoption of the false assumption that it is not efficient); false positive is the opposite error—that of allowing the use of inefficient means, particularly of harmful medication, say one that has adverse side effects. These two terms are synonyms of missed opportunities and of false alarms, respectively. They signify in different ways in defense in attacks. A signal on the military radar screen may be understood as a warning signal or not, say of enemy missiles or airplanes or of a flock of geese or some other phenomenon of no military interest. The wrong reading of a warning signal as neutral is a false negative that puts the battlefield in needless risk. The opposite error, the wrong reading of a neutral signal as a warning and activating the alarms, is a false alarm or a false positive that is inconvenient but lass troublesome. Generally, then, action that may turn out to be a false positive is obviously preferable to one that may turn out to be a false negative. The paradigm case here is the fear of appendicitis: a mistaken assumption that an appendix is ill is preferable to the mistaken assumption that it is healthy: it is better to remove a healthy appendix than to leave an inflamed one unattended, often even a postponement by a day or two may prove fatal. It was thus considered proper to remove healthy appendices. This must have a limit of course, since not every complaint that sound like a sign of appendicitis leads to the removal of an appendix. So if no more than a quarter of the cases in a given department of surgery are needless removals of healthy appendices, the error was deemed tolerable. Of course, the improvement of the diagnostic tools reduced this error rate. It now rests on seven percent or thereabout. It has still not reached zero, and it will probably come nearer to that goal, but perhaps it never will reach it. Moreover, suspecting a case of appendicitis, a family physician may instruct a patient to take a painkiller and return after a few hours if the pain persists. This move is reasonable: it is also subject to false positive and false negative developments, but usually the odds are better when taking it than not. Still, when family physicians have relatively easy access to better means to examine patients for appendicitis, then they ought to use them rather than postpone a decision pending the outcome of the use of a painkiller. However, we must also consider that the use of other means may have high opportunity-costs. That is to say, in some situations the available means may be better used for other ends. This complicates the considerations beyond the scope of the present discussion as it moves from doubts about given diagnoses of given patients to the question of how to optimize the utility of given public services. So we return to false positive and false negative, as disputes about them are simpler and so reducing the frustration that they may cause is also simpler.

Decision theory begins with the commonsense suggestion to write down the list of options open to the individual who has to decide upon a solution to a given relatively pressing problem. This suggestion is so obvious and so inexpensive, that you would take it for granted that people employ it regularly. Instead they do it in their heads. We do not know why, but we do observe the reluctance of ever so many people to use pencil and paper (or a word processor). This reluctance is the result of education, as is obvious from the fact that educators who insist on training their charges to use paper and pencil avoid infecting them with this malady.

Each solution may be true or false (or else there is no decision problem). Each solution has its costs and its benefits once it is true/false and the decision-maker does/does not act on it. In other words, there are four options for each possible solution and each has its costs and its benefits. This is a long list. The first item that a reasonable, responsible decision-maker examines and tries to avoid is the possibility of a cost that is too high, especially if it cannot possibly be defrayed. The problem may be such that this is not in the field of possibilities. The next thing is to divide the errors into the two types that we have mentioned, the false positive and the false negative. It comes handy here, in the commonsense consideration of the decision in question: they are relevant to any technology that under consideration for application. Discussions of the question, which of the possible technologies to invest in, should include investigations of both the expected cost and the expected benefits of false negatives and of false positives.

For example, when considering whether or not it makes sense to invest in the development of an electrical car, we should estimate (1) the expected loss that we will suffer if we invest in developing the car and find out that the investment was a loss, and (2) the expected loss if we refrain from developing the car, leaving its development to competitors who thus corner the market. (Obviously, in this case the expected loss due to investment that turns out to be futile is small in comparison with failure to come up with a superior technology that drives an entrepreneur or a firm altogether out of the market. This is why many corporations allot some funds for research in technologies that do not look promising.)

The calculation of the expected loss is the product of the following two factors:

1. The welfare or utility (for example, the welfare we gain by having electrical car, and the damage we suffer by not having such a car);
2. The likelihood of achieving this welfare (for example, the probability of successfully developing the electrical car).

Consider the question whether or not a government or an entrepreneur should invest in a certain technology, or whether a government should encourage the use of a certain technology, or whether a government should take the risk and allow for a new technology to enter the market. When disputing such questions, two different issues are at stake so that the dispute may be broken down into two features: the estimation of the amount of increase of human welfare due to the successful development of the technology under discussion, and the assessment of the likelihood of success of developing that technology. As these issues are obviously interrelated, many people often mistakenly forego notice of their distinctness. It is advisable to study distinct issues separately and then to correct the results by considering their interdependence. This requires of parties to any dispute to be patient while the considerations are made and wait for their corrections. Just knowing this suffices to reduce considerably any frustration involved.

Some people cannot bring themselves to study issues on obviously erroneous suppositions: they may know that no study can be assured freedom from error, and nevertheless they cannot stand the idea of employing ideas they know are erroneous. This in itself is a great error. Just think of the idea of indirect proof in mathematics. It is the reasoning on a false assumption meant to get to a blind alley: it is having got into a blind alley that is the proof. A bit more complex is the approximation method: seeking a numerical solution to a problem just guess any number; it is almost certain to be false. Take it to be true and work it out and you will find that it is false and even that it is too big or too small. Make your next conjecture in light of this information; if the approximation method works, your results will improve and for practical purposes they do not have to be true: the problem situation prescribes the degree of precision required, that is, the maximal permitted distance between the approximate and the true solution. It sounds odd that it is possible to know if the approximation is sufficiently good or not even without knowing the true solution. But this is sufficiently often the case.

Most engineering projects rest on scientific ideas that are good enough, even though better theories are available that correct some of their errors. The paradigm case here involves studies of flow in hydrodynamics or aerodynamics, which rest on the supposition that the medium (water or air) is continuous, although we know that it is atomic. Moreover, since the supposition is erroneous, some of its conclusions are erroneous too, as for example the conclusion that no airplane can cross the sound barrier. To study this phenomenon, the atomic character of air must enter the considerations.

Back to the two separate issues noted above: regarding a new technology, assessing the likelihood of its success and assessing the increase of welfare that its successful implementation should cause comprise two separate issues, each of which comprises a challenge that is quite difficult. There is no direct way to measure the likelihood of successful development and implementation of an innovation, be it a machine, software or a medication. (Again, this is the case for any act of prospecting.) Having experienced many cases in which overly optimistic engineers failed to meet their predictions, investors and managers increase the margin of error for the budget estimations that they receive from engineers. Nevertheless, all too many projects exceed their budgets despite this measure.

Moreover, in many cases there is also no simple way to measure the welfare or utility that an innovation may bring about. Consider medicine. The utility of a life-saving pill is the value of life. If you say that life is invaluable, namely, that the value of life is infinite, then you must conclude that it makes sense to invest in the development of any pill that might save life, which is clearly impossible. Politicians, physicians, military commanders and even ordinary drivers do consciously risk lives; hence, they do not assign an infinite value even to their own lives. And indeed, some studies comprise efforts to figure out the value that people do assign to their lives; these assessments are based on the estimations of transactions that involve the possible rescue of lives. For an example consider the question of how much money buyers might agree to add to the cost of car in order to increase its safety. The trouble with this exercise is that people do not think of the cost of saving lives (perhaps because they constantly hear that it is infinite) and so their estimations of it vary with the methods by which their answers to the question is elicited.

The estimation of the welfare or utility is even more difficult when we consider environmental protection technology. Here the welfare of future generations enters the equation. And then we must determine how much we discount their welfare, if at all. (The discount rate is the rate of reduction of payment in order to advance the time of its defray.) This question, however, lies beyond the scope of this handbook. All we say here is, to reduce frustration, beware of the pitfalls of considering estimations that efforts to calculate a bit more precisely gets quickly on a reef.

Disputes About Advantages and Drawbacks

We are not done with the cost of saving lives. We have said, there is not enough money to invest in all life-saving projects. This is true but somewhat superficial: to have no money for any commodity means that it has no priority over any commodity for which there is some budget. Thus, when we need some medication and we have no savings, we spend less of our income on some commodity or another in order to have the money needed for the medication. We usually try to reduce consumption of the item in our budget with the least priority. Thus, we usually spend some money on luxury, but when pressed for money we reduce their consumption. The same holds for national budgets, by the way, and the fact that the first budget cuts are from education testifies to the fact that governments take education to be a luxury. Not by considering national needs but party needs; but this is a different matter. Our question here is, why do we spend on luxury, such as cosmetics, when we can use the money spent on them for efforts to save lives? The answer is that we prefer the lifestyle with cosmetics and somewhat lower life expectancy over the lifestyle with no cosmetics and higher life expectancy. To be precise, there is a limit to the reduction of life expectancy that we tolerate, so that when the rate of death on the highway is higher than we tolerate, we increase the budget for highway safety. This shows how complex such questions are and why they are so frustrating. So you should know this before entering disputes about such matters.

Many disputes in the field of technology concern lists of advantages and disadvantages of diverse options (in accord with decision theory, you may remember) rather than disagreement about theories. Consider the dispute regarding whether or not we (the nation or the corporation) should invest in electrical cars. Supporters of this investment list the expected advantages of the use of electrical cars: the reduction of pollution (at least inside big cities), of servicing costs, of dependence on fossil fuel, etc. Opponents to this investment list the drawbacks of electrical cars: batteries are expensive; the span of travel enabled between stops to charge batteries is more limited than between fuel tanking, etc. This procedure is apt for courts of law, you should remember, where advocates for the different sides are expected to be biased since the judge and jury are expected to weigh the differing sides of the argument. This is not true of parties to a dispute within one and the same corporation. Both sides there agree on the list of advantages and the list of drawbacks. They disagree on one or both of the following aspects of the issue:

1. The costs of the advantages and drawbacks, and/or
2. The likelihood of successfully developing technologies that will change these lists and their costs.

These two items may lead different parties to opt for different steps despite their agreement on the advantages and disadvantages of each step. Not knowing this obviously creates immense frustration rooted in impatience. Again, our advice is that you be aware of the situation and see how it prevents frustration or at least reduces it.

The dispute about genetically modified foods may serve as another example. Although the dispute seems like a huge fight, there is a general agreement as to the current advantages of genetically modified food (higher yield, less need for pest control, and more). They disagree, however, about the risk that genetic modification incurs, as, for example, the likelihood that their resistance to disease will transfer from desirable plants to undesirable plants. This is a dispute about the likelihood of future scenarios; it is not a dispute about theories or other generalizations.

Now although genetic engineering could not enter the discussion before the discovery of the genetic code (in the mid-twentieth-century) this is not to say that it was not practiced. It was practiced unknowingly. The latest activity of this kind (of unknowing modifying genera) is the use of antibiotics. But many other activities interfere with our ability to survive, and some of them are genetically transmitted, including our changing of our environment, our diverse medical technologies (including immunization), and more. This leads to some precaution measures when these are not too expensive, such as keeping in store seeds of all sorts of vegetation and even semen of living things, especially humans. This may sound frustrating but it does the opposite as it reduces the pressure of conservative arguments in favor of avoiding certain kinds of innovations, since innovation is unavoidable and we never know what it brings on its wings.

In the field of technology, only a few extant disputes fall outside the patterns depicted here. One such example is the dispute about how much governments should invest in space research by launching human-occupied space shuttles. One party says that such space shuttles are too expensive, and contribute almost nothing to scientific research relative to spaceships run by remote control. The other party claims that we must concentrate on sending people to outer space in order to conquer it sometime in the not too distant future. Both parties agree about the advantages and drawbacks of each technology, and they even agree as to the costs involved. The disagreement then rests on the targets of research into outer-space, and in this sense this disagreement is not about technology but rather about the targets for the future of human society.

Global Warming II

We have already discussed the debate about global warming in Chap. 5. We reviewed there the debate about the question, whether the world become warmer, and if so, why. We will now turn to the next question: What is the best way to reduce the risk of global warming?

Wishing to develop the discussion a bit further, we have to estimate the costs of two scenarios—the scenario that global warming continues and the damages to human society will be as severe as the students of climate change predict (that is the cost of a miss), versus the scenario that we will drastically cut the pollution, and eventually will discover that there was no need for this (the cost of false alarm). The difference between the damages in these two scenarios is huge.

The problem is much more complex, since once we decide to take steps in order to reduce global warming by reducing pollution from fossil fuels and by other methods, the next question is, how much effort and money should be allocated to effect this reduction, and when should we start. Remember: the effort and money that are allocated to war against global warming could be used for other good purposes such as reducing poverty.

These considerations lead us to disputes about ethic and politics which are the subject of the next chapter.

Chapter 10
Disputes About Ethics and Politics

Abstract When debating moral questions, it is advisable to consider the extent to which each view rests on sympathizing with the suffering of others versus the extent to which its adoption rests on the hope that acting on it will increase human welfare. Such understanding can help clarify some rather abstract notions that might otherwise disrupt such debates.

The field of ethics and politics is known as that of proposals and decisions—perhaps together with aesthetics. Yet aesthetic considerations are less burdened with considerations for other people and with one's ability to interfere with other people's lives: unlike ethical and political decisions, the aesthetic one seldom causes pain to other people, at least not the way moral and political decisions can.

This is not quite true. There is one decision that is paramount in any individuals' life that concerns chiefly that individual's well-being, and it pertains to ethics, politics and aesthetics. It is the matter of one's own choice of a lifestyle. Let us discuss this for a short while before turning to the rest of the theory of proposals and decisions.

The Choice of a Lifestyle

The most important decision available to every individual is that of the choice of a lifestyle. Since the options are too many, we should limit our discussion to available lifestyles to choose from. These are limited first and foremost by our abilities: most of us have to earn a living and most of us cannot become professionals in ever so many fields: one is able to be a professional in one field and another in another. Nor is it all: some of us would enter a profession that is satisfying despite poor remunerations, and others prefer remuneration to satisfaction. These are personal choices, and the standard advice that all wise advisors offer is that we remember that many people find in the eve of their lives that they have made the wrong choice, so that it is advisable to think carefully about this matter. Now this advice, to think carefully, is not very useful. It is easy, however, to translate it to a practical proposal: try to engage in debates with advisers who disagree with each other and continue debates that do not frustrate you. Some advisors specialize in the choice of profession, others in matters religious or other common matters. Choose different kinds of advisors and, again, of different persuasions. And, remember, you are the best judge about what debate to continue and what to truncate.

Since we are social animals, our options are largely determined by available options in every society and by available societies. Since migration is a very radical option, and since it is open to very few, we can dispense with it right away: one need not decide on it in one go: more often one moves to another country for a specific reason and stays there only after further decision, given the options that open up in due course.

The most significant choice is of one's lifestyle in a very personal sense: should one choose to be socially active? Should one decide to live by high moral standard or will one be content with being of average virtue. And so on. On this the slogan of Socrates signifies most. It is, *the unexamined life is not worth living*. And the examination he recommended is, of course, by dialogue. We will say no more on this except that it holds with particular force in our contemporary society, where there is more social freedom than ever before, and where religious freedom enables one to decide on one's religious affiliation and practice as never before. And of course, one always has the choice of political affiliation and practice as never before. We are now moving to the fields of ethics and politics, with proposals as to what rule may help us most in fruitful and enjoyable debates in these fields.

Criteria for Ethics and Politics

Many disputes refer to questions in ethics and politics, such as:

1. To what extent should we help the poor?
2. What is the best system of governance?
3. When it is morally permissible / imperative to lie?

Philosophers concerned with ethics have traditionally searched for methods to measure the plausibility of moral judgments. However, skeptical considerations lead to the conclusion that no such method exists. (For skepticism see Appendix.) If any moral judgment follows from this it is fallibilism: we have to learn to live in uncertainty and we should try to make our lives as good as we can even though we will never know if we have succeeded, since no (moral) judgment is certain or fully plausible, no (moral) knowledge is ever available, and no (moral) judgment can be fully justified. Hence, a valid method for the resolution of ethical disputes by measuring the plausibility of the judgments of the disputed sides is likewise impossible.

Still, in many cases people agree about ethical issues and many moral disputes end in agreement, whether certainty in moral judgments exists or not. Admittedly, unanimity is no criterion of correctness. For example, for millennia there was unanimity about slavery, and when the first anti-slavery movement began, its members were dismissed as obviously unrealistic. Moral agreement, thus, often rests on agreements on matters of fact, and the views agreed upon are often false and even silly. Indeed, ever so much traditional moral agreement concern gender and sex, and they are quite silly, as today we easily agree. Leaving factual judgments aside, we observe that moral agreement is often due to shared psychological traits described well enough in two principles. They are as follows.

1. The sympathy principle (David Hume's principle): We sympathize with the suffering of others and we do consider it immoral to perform any act that increases it needlessly.
2. The welfare principle: Were we able, we would gladly legislate for the whole of humanity rules that would optimize human welfare.

We tend to sympathize with the sufferings of others. This is a psychological disposition that almost all of us share, even if to varying degrees. Those who lack this disposition totally we deem defective; we consider them immoral or rather a-moral, unable to possess moral sentiment or judgment. We thus view their defect as pathology, psychological or social.

Notably, we sympathize not only with humans but also with other animals. This disposition explains the efforts of some thinkers and their followers who advocate animal rights. Admittedly, they are the exception. Yet we all share with them the idea that animals have some moral rights: we all agree that torturing animals for fun is immoral and we all support the laws that forbid making animals suffer needlessly, not always in detail but always in principle.

The disposition to sympathize has evolved slowly over eons. For example, to repeat, until recently slavery was taken as morally permissible as a matter of course; significantly, this is no longer the case. We explain this as a result of the growth of our ability to sympathize. In the past, slave owners considered slaves not quite human, at least not human "like us". Indeed, whenever the sympathy with slaves grew, it became ever more desirable to enslave only others. We have as a prominent example the transition period, in which slaves of our own tribe were kept only for a limited period, and only slaves of other tribe were kept for good. This is recorded in Scriptures. It says (*Exodus* 21:2), *"If you buy a Hebrew slave, he is to serve for only six years."* A later version seems to forbid this altogether, saying (*Leviticus* 25:44), *"you may purchase male or female slaves from among the foreigners who live among you"*. In the United States in the last stage of slavery all slaves were deemed black, even though most of them were of mixed ancestry, and they were declared not-human, of pre-Adamite descent, created before Adam. We refer to this folly as means of suppression of sympathy, as was the vulgar derogatory expression "nigger-lover" that came to replace the older "Jew-lover".

The sympathy principle is insufficient for proper morality. It does not explain, for example, why breaking promises is reprehensible, and why charity is commendable. This is where the second principle enters, the welfare principle: we advocate keeping promises and donating to charity just because we expect such acts to increase welfare. Indeed, those who in principle oppose all charity—socialists and anarchists of all sorts—explain their opposition by the argument that despite good intentions and despite impression to the contrary, charity reduced welfare. The question of whether they are right is very important, of course; in the present discussion, however, it is not, as it is but an illustration for our claim that arguments for or against the characterization of this or that mode of conduct as moral or immoral often rests on estimates of resultant welfare. It is, indeed, hard to identify the effect of charity, since clearly its immediate consequences are favorable: it raises welfare visibly at once. Opponents say that in the long run it reduces welfare, since charity competes with other arrangements to alleviate suffering and its application reduces likelihood of the implementation of these arrangements, whatever they may be. This is a dangerous argument, since in some cases immediate charity saves lives, and it is impossible to improve the welfare of the dead. Nevertheless, people argue this way, adding that even the immediate outcome of charity is tainted, since the right to live in dignity is immediate and charity deprives its recipient of this. At this point we have to stop reporting on this discussion as it gets too intricate to serve as mere illustration.

Here a new idea has sneaked in: the right for dignity. We in the modern world live in welfare states, since every modern state provides for its needy citizens one way or another. A strong movement in contemporary society opposes welfare but not charity. Sometime this movement was called Raeganism, after the United-States President Ronald Reagan, who was elected on an anti-welfare-state platform. He repeatedly stressed that his opposition was not to welfare but to the state bureaucracy that runs welfare institutions, including the great institution of social security. He said, let churches and other non-governmental organizations run the welfare system, not the state. Supporters of the welfare state said, if the government bureaucracy is too heavy, then it needs overhaul, but not at the expense of the citizen. The citizen's right for welfare is no charity; it is the right to life with dignity. We do not intend to resolve this dispute here; we use this as an example of the force and the popularity of our second principle: those who wish the dispute resolved one way or another—and being a practical matter it calls for a resolution—have one tool to apply to that end: the welfare principle: comparing the assignment of the tasks of caring for the welfare of the citizen to the government with its assignment to non-government organizations (NGOs), which of the two causes a greater increase to human welfare in general?

Let us stress this: our psychological theory cannot replace ethics with psychology, nor is it meant to do that. This handbook concerns disputes, not ethics. For our purposes of helping the facilitating disputes, our psychological theory is relevant in this chapter as a means for helping resolve some sorts of moral disputes. Indeed, we generally advise that if and when a debate about factual issues may replace moral issues with no party to the dispute complaining, then they should attempt to do this for a while—but reverse the change if it starts frustrating any participant. (This advice, let us notice, clashes with our advice to be patient. This clash is general and unavoidable. It therefore calls for good sense, for tentative judgments and decisions that seem reasonable.)

To render practical our suggestion to render moral disputes factual, let us add this. Moral disputes can be rendered factual in at least three ways.

1. Different parties have different intuitions regarding sympathizing with the suffering of others.
2. Different parties have different views as to what means are best for enhancing human welfare.
3. One party's intuitions regarding sympathy conflict with the other party's intuitions regarding the means for increasing welfare.

As an example of the first case, consider disputes about the morality of abortion. Indeed, in this case, as in many other cases, sympathy with fetuses plays a central role: some sympathize with fetuses, viewing them as people, and others do not, viewing them as no different from brain-dead individuals. A dispute that results from a disagreement about sympathy might lead the disputing parties to attempts to find arguments showing that the object of the contested sympathy does or does not resemble humans like themselves. When discussing the morality of abortion, then, they may try to determine how similar human fetuses are to full-fledged humans. Indeed, the major tool in the hands of anti-abortionists is the illustration of the similarity between fetuses and babies.

Disputes about sexual freedom can serve as examples for the second case. Those who oppose such freedom take it for granted that it threatens the survival of society, and those who favor it disagree on this. (The advocates of sexual freedom may also claim that it increases human welfare. But they need not do that, since in our contemporary liberal society the onus is on the party that demands restrictions on freedom to argue that the constraint is necessary. So it is up to the advocates of sexual freedom to decide whether to demand sexual freedom or to merely oppose constraints on it. Of course, this way they argue for liberalism as a moral principle. It also rests on the welfare principle as advocated here. The difference between these two debate strategies becomes important if anyone argues that constraints on sexual conduct is needed not only for the welfare of society in general but also to protect some weak individuals form some suffering that sexual freedom may inflict on them.)

The advantage of replacing a moral dispute with a factual dispute is obvious. It gets to the root of the disagreement, and it offers better chances for resolutions. Thus, a dispute that results from a disagreement about a theory concerning human welfare might bring the parties to it to attempts to test that theory scientifically. For example, they can test the theory that free sex risks the survival of society. To repeat, one may claim that society might benefit from this phenomenon: its advocates should then seek scenarios in which different kinds of sexual codes are beneficial or detrimental to a society or to its individual members. For, it is indeed generally agreed that every change has both positive and negative aspects. Moreover, we should repeat our observation.

A new factor enters the theory of disputation here. Whatever a dispute is, we stress, it is no longer reasonable to defend the conservative attitude that favors the *status quo* for fear of change alone. Traditional society needs reform badly as it treats too many people (mostly women and children) too cruelly, while the modern world makes too many traditional customs no longer viable. So propaganda for any social reform as opposed to the defense of the *status quo* has become one-sided. The same goes for propaganda for uncontroversial cases, such as those of child abuse and child pornography, where the scenarios have become almost entirely one-sided. To be effective, all scenarios should be specific, detailed, and, above all honest. One-sided writers of scenarios are not forced to be as cautious as those who write against powerful opponents. So they will do well to remember that and keep vigil against self-deception. And, to repeat another observation of ours, mere preaching against self-deception is of little value unless it is boosted by the assertion that the best means for this is to invite honest criticism, and the best incentive for this is that nothing is better than criticism for learning and improving and growing.

Finally, the dispute about the morality of economic globalization serves us as an example of the third case. Like all reforms, globalization too has its victims. Many people sympathize with the suffering of these victims, among them certain European farmers. This sympathy is expressed in moral intuitions that may (rightfully or not) lead to opposition to globalization. A different moral intuition yields support for globalization. It usually stems from the fact that globalization facilitates the flow of capital to poor countries that need it badly, plus the endorsement of neo-classical economic theory that presents free trade as a promise of rapid increase of welfare all round. To resolve this kind of dispute, the parties might attempt to clarify the source of the difference (the sympathy principle and the welfare principle) and spell out the arguments in sufficient detail to be able to discuss them critically and reassess them in the hope of approaching agreement. The details of such a discussion easily proliferate and we will not discuss them here. Let us mention only that in general, when some economic reform causes pain to some individuals, it is worthwhile to compensate them handsomely. If this compensation is difficult for economic reasons, then the economic reform is not economic enough. We say this as we find that economists are not always as disinterested as they imply when they claim scientific status for their ideas on the tacit understanding that it is foolish to contest a received scientific idea. In any case, such claims are beside the point, as the dispute belongs to applied science, not to science proper.

Our presentation does not cover all cases of moral dispute, of course, since our examples are of cases where the nub of the moral disagreement may be factual. Some moral disputes are different. Consider revenge. Some people find revenge morally justifiable. Obviously, it does not follow from the sympathy principle (neither sympathy with the attacker nor sympathy with the victim), nor does it follow from the welfare principle (as an act of destruction, revenge as such cannot possibly increase the welfare of humanity). Hence, in a dispute about revenge (should one take revenge, and if so, under what conditions and with what means?), it makes sense to check if both parties agree that revenge is morally justifiable. Disagreement about this question makes it premature to argue about the type and the scope of the revenge. It seems to us that revenge is slowly disappearing from our moral maps, which is all for the better for many reasons. We also explain this phenomenon by the views, common among anthropologists, that feuds are the only means for administering justice in primitive societies. Notice that this is relevant to the discussion about revenge, as the feud is a kind of revenge. Hence, those who advocate revenge may agree to include in the discussion about the morality of revenge the idea of the feud and its function in decentralized society. This will be the appeal to the welfare principle, so that we need not expand on it here.

Noticing that the feud has advantage over modern system of justice as it needs no administrators, operating as it does with no police and no judges, may sound irrelevant to moral disputes about revenge, since in primitive society it is the only system available and so it is commendable there, whereas it has no function in modern society and so it is immoral here. This seems to us quite possible, yet not conclusive. We see traces of feud in organized societies. (Thus, biblical law tolerates feuds nut limits them.) Hence, possibly, this shows that the problem is possibly more complex. So one may claim that survival of primitive customs is unavoidable and so ethics should take this into account. This is a mix of a factual and a moral claim. Both aspects of it, incidentally, gain support from the existentialist theory of authenticity: we should be honest with ourselves and admit that we are still primitive. This is primitivism. True to our advice, we will tackle here its factual component. Not only is the renunciation of slavery an argument against this primitivism. The passion for dueling is a stronger example. It is well known that despite legal proscription of it, dueling survived into the twentieth century. Yet these days it is laughable. The same holds for the hostility to homosexuality that waned ever since Lord John Wolfenden's 1957 Report of the Departmental Committee on Homosexual Offences and Prostitution declared its widespread and today they win recognition that was unimaginable only a half-a-century ago.

We should conclude this point by saying this. We do not know what human nature is and what traits of it are such the any reasonable moral theory should admit them. Suffice it to say that since this is not obvious, it is open to debates. If debates will not do, then perhaps the diverse arts can help by inducing sympathy and by ridiculing defunct customs. And there is nothing like old works of art to show us how much our moral sentiment has evolved. Yet we should repeat our caveat: art settles no dispute even if at times it can provide terrific arguments in favor of one party and against the other. To show this let us show that the theory of revenge does not leave the scene without trace even as it gives way to its replacement, the theory of social responsibility and the legal system.

We show this by the example of an argument that does not fall under our two principles. It concerns the responsibility of individuals for actions of members of their (small) families. How responsible are the offspring of Nazis who participated in crimes against humanity? To what extent are they to blame for their parents' crimes? This is not a matter of guilt. It is more practical. Should the offspring compensate the surviving victims of their parents' crimes? Once again an answer to this question (be it positive or negative) follows from neither the sympathy nor the welfare principle. Indeed, before entering disputes about such questions, it makes sense to examine whether both parties agree or disagree on the principle that families are responsible for some crimes of their members. This dispute is not much different from the previous dispute, about the morality or immorality of feuds, yet it belongs to the law of torts, not quite to ethics.

We can generalize this. Traditional ethics seeks for the justification of the right morality. It centers on the possibility of justification before it goes into discussions of the question, what are the right rules of morality? We gave up the search for justification and we seek the right rules. We confess ignorance and claim that this question is on the agenda for debate. Is that moral on our part? How? Yes. And on the principle that it is a moral imperative to confess ignorance and seek to remedy it. We claim that this is a moral imperative. Moreover, we contend that we cannot improve our views on morality without considering the factual issues that ethics involved, at times issues to resolve by natural science and technology, more often by social, especially political considerations. This we introduced obliquely through the welfare principle. This is not enough as the previous paragraph illustrates. We have to do so more directly. Let us move then from ethics to politics. Before that let us make two final observations on ethics.

As we have noted, people change their minds about morality, at times for the better. We already mentioned a few examples of practices that many societies considered morally permissible and now most of them consider immoral. We have neglected one very important example: torture. Not long ago, torturing criminals was considered morally permissible (perhaps as revenge, perhaps as a necessary evil). Now, many people concur that this practice is immoral and international conventions forbid it. Our moral sense as human beings has grown and will hopefully continue to grow.

That morals improve may be taken for granted, but a very popular philosophy says the opposite: moral relativism. Beware of moral relativism: it is the view that all moral views are equally justifiable or equally unjustifiable. A paradigm example is clitoridectomy or female circumcision. Many moral relativists claim that in the societies in which it is practiced it is moral. Entering a dispute about moral questions with those that hold this view is useless and frustrating. Do not confuse our hypotheses about morality being forever fallible with moral relativism. We assert that some psychological tendencies that most people share (the sympathy and welfare principles) may facilitate some moral disputes and render them more reasonable. This view recognizes the possibility of moral growth, unlike (moral) relativism that does not, as the view that all (moral) views are equally justifiable blocks any dispute about moral questions and voids all incentive to improve morality. Debating with relativists is bound to bring about nothing but frustration.

Politics

Many disputes refer to politics, and many political debates deal with specific and with general questions:

1. When does / should the government undertake a certain kind of activity?
2. What is the best system of governance?

When discussing such questions, it is advisable for the contending parties to take into account considerations of the kind mentioned in the previous chapter (on disputes on matters technological) regarding the cost and benefits of false negatives and of false positives. To repeat, when the question arises as to whether a certain scientific theory is true, one option is to not to answer it. We can simply say that we do not know; abstaining from commitment need not incur great cost. This option is not always present in discussions of political issues: these belong to practice, not to theory; to technology, not to science. When governments consider given options to decide upon, they face two kinds of potential damages: (1) the chosen activity is useless or worse yet the government decides to apply it; and (2) the activity is useful and possibly even vital yet the government decides not to apply it. When debating potential government activities, both such kinds of damages should be considered.

As with disputes on other matters technological, in many political debates, disputing parties may agree about the possible merits and risks of the activity under dispute. The disagreement in these cases rests on their estimation of the likelihood of success and on the value of the success or failure in question, namely the resultant increase or decrease in public welfare. Therefore, to resolve such disputes, it makes sense to list the components of the disagreement, so that the parties can see what exactly is at issue.

Consider disputes about taxes. One party proposes to raise a certain tax; another party demands that the proposed tax be reduced or even abolished. Criteria for good taxes are easy to list: they should not have too many undesirable qualities such as raising inequality (they should be progressive), they should not encumber collection (preferably they should employ existing means for collection), and they should not disturb economic activity (they should not reduce productivity). Unfortunately, no tax mechanism would fully meet all these criteria. Therefore, when discussing whether a certain new tax is desirable and should be legislated, or whether an existing tax is to be abolished, it makes sense to evaluate its advantages and its disadvantages according to some agreed-upon criteria, such as the criteria mentioned above. As long as the criteria are agreed upon, the dispute involves evaluating how much the tax under discussion meets the criteria (in comparison with alternatives). This is not a dispute about theories or generalizations, but rather about measures. Such disputes are often very frustrating because parties to them do not check whether they employ the same criteria or not. If neither party has a criterion, the debate can proceed nevertheless; it is when criteria are different, yet each party is convinced that their criterion is the obvious one to employ in that dispute, that frustration is assured.

In discussions of changes in current policies, another issue regularly arises: the fear that the change would result in excessive social and political disorder (or in a significant deterioration of the current situation), bringing about needless suffering. In particular, fear repeatedly emerges that great changes in governance bring about chaos. This may be explained by the application of the economic or quasi-economic idea known as the law of diminishing marginal utility. The suffering caused by the loss of one dollar depends on the current amount of money in one's possession: the richer one is, the less one suffers from the loss of one dollar. Thus, the expected pleasure from gain must be smaller than the expected suffering from loss. Hence, it makes no sense to take a bet with even chances of gaining or losing the same amount of money. Now, since changes in governance may fail (and we learn from history that regrettably this happens all too often), this law makes it sensible to initiate a change in any system of government only when the suffering that the current system incurs is excessive and if the expected gain from the change is reasonably higher than the potential loss from it would be, or if the injustice it is expected to rectify and pain it is expected to reduce is considerably greater than the injustice and pain that it might unwittingly engender. In this sense, under normal conditions, as Karl Popper has observed, some degree of conservatism may be rational and it may be advisable to set the default option, which would be upset only in cases of urgency, in cases of great social distress or risk, and in cases of significant opportunity.

This explains why the seventeenth century thinkers who have inaugurated modern political philosophy repeatedly endorsed powerful monarchies, even though today many consider such political systems downright immoral. Indeed, even the British public, for a conspicuous example, supports the British constitutional monarchy but would likely admit that had they live in a republic, they would not advocate monarchy, much less an automatically transmitted one with no control mechanisms.

The strongest argument for conservatism is that even the best reform takes much effort to implement, whereas current self-supporting systems require no investment of effort to run. Let us repeat, whether this argument is valid or not does not signify any more since we no longer live in a world that is so stable that we have to think twice before reforming it. We have declared World War I and World War II and have found ourselves in an increasingly unstable world that requires serious global reforms for it to survive. This idea developed before the great threats to human survival developed: it is a part of the Charter of the United Nations. Unfortunately, this Charter has proven not good enough and not strong enough. Yet it was not total failure. Its Declaration of Human Rights stand out as a fine achievement despite all frustrations.

Human Rights

Some disputes refer to cases that relate to conflicting human rights. For example, the right to free speech may conflict with the right to privacy or with national security, leading to the dispute of which takes precedence. Following our principles, we suggest that rights are useful as a kind of shortcuts, since usually we cannot calculate the expected influence of actions upon the welfare of all citizens. Therefore, to resolve such disputes, it makes sense to judge these rights and their relative weights on the basis of empirical hypotheses about the best way for legislation to raise welfare and test these hypotheses in accord with received rules. Similarly, in disputes about questions pertaining to the enactments of new laws concerning rights, opponents may try to refute claims that such laws increase welfare.

All this squares with the claim that the greatest achievement concerning human rights is their very endorsement, as a part of international and global politics. It sounds too smug to brag about the laws of human rights despite their frequent violations. Yet the fact remains, human rights organizations (including Amnesty International) demand that even tyrannical regimes endorse, say, conventions against torture, even though obviously undertaking to avoid torture does not stop tyrants from torturing dissidents. This leads to many questions that should be debated. Debates on such practical matters may improve moral conduct and so they are superior to discussing ethics in the traditional mode. We hope that these words will move some of our readers to try and improve philosophy curricula.

The Problem of Inequality

We will end this chapter by reviewing a few problems that are debated in many forums. The first example is the debate on questions of inequality. In what follows we will suggest how this debate should be conducted.

The first stage is formulating a question as an interrogative sentence. Below are some possible examples:

1. What is inequality?

To repeat, we suggest avoiding "what is" questions. Indeed, there are various methods of measuring inequality, and rather than ask which the real one is, we can discuss the success or failure to deliver the goods. For example, one method measures inequality by the difference of gross domestic product (GDP) per person, another method measures the Purchasing Power Parity (PPP) which takes into account the differences among the prices in each place. Still other measures the welfare by taking into account education and health. But this is a technical question, and the parties to the debate should agree upon it in advance. They may also agree to use several methods in parallel. (All this the theory at the background to "what is" questions renders impossible.)

Another popular formulation is:

2. Should we decrease inequality between people?

This question might be debated only if at least one of the disputing parties sincerely thinks that inequality is a virtue. Most people—and most politicians—do not think so. At least as a default position, most people claim that large inequality is bad, and that therefore we should try to reduce it, as long as we do not reduce other qualities that we deem virtuous.

A better formulation is:

3. What is the best way to decrease inequality?

This formulation assumes that inequality, at least excessive inequality, is harmful, and this assumption is quite common. It is an important question since it implies that the government, and thus also each of us, should do something about it.

Note however that it makes sense to distinguish between two questions:

4. What is the best way to decrease inequality in a given country?
5. What is the best way to decrease inequality between nations?

Both questions are important.

The list of answers to question (4) includes:

The government should levy more taxes from the rich people and transfer money to the poor.

The government should administer cheap, high-quality services such as education and health.

Note that one of the possible answer is: decrease the standard of living of the entire population and increase corruption of the government. This is an easy practical way that results in more harm than benefit. We do not mean this. Hence, we want to increase equality without reducing the standard of living. This we do not say as we take it as self-understood. It is one party to a dispute taking a point as self-understood and the other not that assures frustration.

A similar list of answers refers to question (5) and obviously there are many more possible answers.

The debate about these answers leads to additional questions in sociology, economics, psychology and ethics. Here are some obvious examples.

If the government raises the taxes on the rich, will many of them move to another country? If so, can we prevent this by legislating global taxation?

Does supply of free services lead to laziness? If so, should the government avoid supplying free services to the able-bodied?

Which situation is morally better, small inequality coupled with relatively low standard of living, or high inequality coupled with a high average standard of living?

National Rights

The second example refers to the debates about national rights. Many people in world demand a state for their nation, while other object these demands. The Catalans and the Basks in Spain, the Kurds in Iraq and the Palestinians in Israel are some famous examples. The disputes about these demands are furious. We suggest the following guidelines how to handle such disputes rationally.

Woodrow Wilson, USA's President during the First World War, promoted the principle that nations should have the "unmolested opportunity of autonomous development". A nation should have an independent state if it can survive by its own means, adopt a democratic regime, and keep the human rights of its minorities.

Does this principle imply that the Catalans the Basks the Kurds or the Palestinians have independent states?

You might start with the question: Are they nations? And then you may go on and ask, what is the definition of nation? Beware of this question. As we mentioned in Chap. 3 disputes about definition are usually frustrating. There is no accepted definition of nation. Allegedly, a group of people that share the same language and culture are a nation. But the people of Switzerland are an obvious counter example (they people of this nation do not share one language) and the people of Australia and the USA are another counter example (two nations with the same language). There are paradigm cases of nations, for example, no one disputes that the French or German are nations. But there are many borderline cases as well: What is the nation of Jews in the USA – the nations of the Jews in Israel or the American nations (or both)? Are the Palestinians a nation? They claim they are, but their national awareness is quite new.

Following the suggestions in Chap. 10 a better way to handle such disputes might be to ask:

If the Kurds in Iraq get an independent state, (1) will it harm other people with whom we sympathize? (2) Will it increase the welfare of the Kurds and their neighbors increase? (3) Will the transition to an independent state cause social disorder?

These questions avoid the dispute about the definition of nation, and concentrate on the target that leads us in ethic and politics.

Note also that when discussing this kind of questions, it makes sense to check not just the standards options (the Kurds should / should not have an independent states) but other options, such as dissolving the nation-state all over the world. This idea was raised early in the twentieth century by Russell and Einstein. They recommended the establishment of a world government, of one state for the entire globe. The European Union is going in this direction, but obviously not in as extreme a fashion as Russell had hoped. This option, like the other options, should be considered according to the above-mentioned three questions.

Global Politics

The abstract political discussions are always hampered by the fact that all divisions of the world into tribes, societies, nations, or states, are fairly *ad hoc*. This does not hamper practical problems, since these are given quite *ad hoc* to begin with. Some people take this to be immoral. Thus, the leading early twentieth-century German-Jewish journalist Walter Benjamin found the Zionism of Martin Buber immoral and contrary to the socialism that they shared. Buber found this position of Benjamin rather silly, since it is easy to evade the demanding immediate local problem by hiding behind engagement with global problems that one can do very little about. If one wants to be active, one has to start somewhere.

This changed after World War II. All of a sudden, humanity was found able to destroy itself and perhaps even all life on earth. There are four possible ways for this: the ability to wage global nuclear war by the **P**roliferation of nuclear weapons, by **P**ollution, by increased **P**overty, and by the possible **P**opulation explosion (the four P's). Clearly, these four factors reinforce each other, clearly, they are not given to local solutions, and, clearly, they are already causing havoc in the migration pressure that they generate.

What is to be done about these problems is a difficult question. As it becomes increasingly pressing, it becomes increasingly difficult to postpone discussing them. For more see Joseph Agassi, *Technology: Philosophical and Social aspects*, 1985.

Popular Political Principles and Styles

Other than personal matters, the topic of most debates is politics. The reason is painfully obvious: politics includes everything that is of public concern. What is of public concern is naturally of great political dispute. Some say, the citizen's welfare or education, is of public concern; others say it is not, except when Big Brother is in control. Some say, even the widespread or scarcity of patriotism is of public concern, and there are illiberal ways of imposing it and liberal ways of remedying the situation so as to make patriotism more palatable. All this is fodder for much public debate.

The most popular political attitude or style is conservatism; it has the backing of the most forceful political principles: conservatism. The conservatives observe a few very common and quite imposing principles. First, individuals learn their mother-tongues and adopt their fathers' professions (notice the dreadful sexism of this expression), and this fixes most of their character. Second, when in Rome, do as the Romans do—or else you do not count and you will scarcely survive. Third, individuals cannot survive without society but society survives in every individual. Fourth and last, tradition is the fund of the experience of the whole society.

It is thus not surprising that most societies are conservative and take their conservative political attitudes for granted, hardly noticing them. This is obvious from the vast literature on social anthropology (that deals mostly with preliterate societies, leaving the modern, industrial society that is left for sociology to study, and the rest to social history, the classics, and so on). The vast anthropological literature has nothing to report about disagreements and less to report about disputes. This explains the conservative conduct of these societies: they have no legislatures and no idea of progress. They do have public bodies that make public decisions, though, especially about war with neighbors. Nevertheless, changes in all societies do occur now and then, even in the most conservative societies. These happen due to wars or to demographic changes or even due to (usually unplanned) innovations—about techniques of war, of irrigation, and more. The invention of the cannon, to mention the paradigm case, has destroyed city walls and thus brought about far-reaching social changes; living outside the city walls brought about myriads of unintended consequences.

The debate about conservative views and practices began with the invention of a new political philosophy—in Greece and more so in early modern Western Europe. The most serious criticism of conservatism is from the injustices that all social systems sanction except for utopia, and utopia does not exist. The case repeatedly reported is the requirement to kill all people dangerous to social stability, including all pretenders to a throne, regardless of their own views or values. This happens in Greek tragedy: whatever the characters do, they are bound to be in the wrong. Yet Greek tragedy deviates from conservatism: in the end of his Oresteia, Aeschylus forces the *Erinyes* or the furies—the local deities of vengeance of Greek mythology—to become the *Eumenides*, the kindly ones. The same holds for Romeo and Juliet who are as innocent as can be yet must die. The novelty of Shakespeare's play is in its conclusion. After the heroes die, at the moment of catharsis, when by tradition the curtain should go down, Shakespeare stops the curtain, forces the elders of the Capulets and the Montagues and makes them say, this cannot be; a change must happen. The question all this raises for conservatives is how much may they sacrifice for the sake of socials stability and under what conditions?

Radicals find defects in conservative social life and wish to replace traditional society with rationally planned one. Which naturally is a Utopia. The first and most significant criticism of conservatism is the observation that differences between societies are accidental, that my having been born to this or that society, and to this or that religious community, is no sufficient reason for my staying there: I have a choice and the choice should be rational. To this end we should ignore all the political ideas that we find and design new, rational ones. This is radicalism. Radicals can be more or less radical in their adoption of more accepted ides or less. This may be a matter of accident: the rule by which an idea is endorsed or rejected is that of rationality and is independent of conservative attitudes to it. The most important traditional item that radicals cannot avoid adopting is the mother tongue. Efforts were made to do away with it too, by the plan to devise a universal language. (Leibniz called it *characteristica universalis*, but he did not invent it: some cabbalists did.) The first effort to develop such a language were made by the leading logicians Gottlob Frege, David Hilbert, Giuseppe Peano and Bertrand Russell. The language in its standard full-fledged version is presented in Principia Mathematica of Russell and Alfred North Whitehead. It is at the base of all computer languages. One cannot possibly use it in ordinary conversation or even in scientific discourse, let alone in live disputes. For this we need a new political principle. Ludwik Zamenhof tries another method—he invented a new "natural" language, Esperanto. It is a simplified Latin akin to the Latino sine flexion of the great mathematician Giuseppe Peano (at times referred to as Peano's Interlingua) but much more user friendly, so that everyone would learn to speak it with little preparation. It did succeed that way, but it never came close to becoming truly widespread. The current alternative is the United Nation's Organization recognition of five languages as its official languages, based on the number of people who use them: English, French, Spanish, Russian and Chinese. (Strictly speaking, as Chinese is a written language, not a spoken one, the language that the United Nation Organization recognizes is

Standard Chinese or simplified Chinese that is a modification of *Pǔtōnghuà* or the Mandarin dialect).

The new political principle that allows for debates is democracy. Now some limited debates occurred even in tyrannies, and historically these led to even increasing democratization. Spinoza has observed that since no stable regime can rely on sheer power, there is some consent in every stable regime, and so democracy is a matter of degree. He advocated as extreme a democracy as possible, and as liberal as possible. How much is possible is a matter of constant debate. The important idea is to introduce liberalism into the debate. Many identify it with toleration. Now, admittedly, the desired or permissible degree of toleration is also a matter of debate, and clearly, liberalism is tolerant. Yet, liberalism is not the same as toleration. Historically there were always regimes that were more tolerant or less, long before the idea of liberalism was invented. Its inventor, Niccolò Machiavelli, presented it as the proposal to avoid making laws that are difficult to abide by and to prefer making laws that would bring citizens to be law-abiding out of self-interest.

Liberalism is now practiced in almost all advanced contemporary societies, so that there is great incentive to view it as profitable. It was not like that when it was first proposed: it was a vision. The question is often raised and avidly discussed as to how liberal can a society be and what kind of liberalism it forbids. More so the cost of liberalism is discussed, especially by anti-liberals who claim that the cost of liberalism is the encouragement of egotism and thus its growth, to the detriment of higher value and with the result of the waning of the community and the subsequence growth of alienation. This too is a favorite topic of debates. It can be great fun and it can be frustrating. To keep it going well one needs to add arguments to both advocates of liberalism and to their opponents. On the whole, this holds for most prolonged debates.

Thus far we covered briefly traditional countries and contemporary countries. This is a gross simplification, since most of the world is neither. The most Important half-way countries, mainly in eastern Asia, such as Singapore and China, present a method that is conservative and authoritative, but still leave big part of economy to the free market, and promotes meritocracy when hiring the civil service employees. (For more detail see Joseph Agassi and Ian C. Jarvie, "A Study in Westernization", in I. C. Jarvie, editor, Hong Kong: A Society in Transition, 1969 and in their Rationality: The Critical View, 1987).

To complicate matters, there is a third party, the reactionaries. Unlike traditionalism the reaction appears only as a reaction to radicalism, and radicalism, to repeat, is characteristically Western. Reactionaries do not wish to preserve current society but hanker after the old regime, the one that has preceded radicalism. To make things more complex, in societies whose traditions are radical, predominantly the United States of America, has its traditionalism to some extent individualist and radical. Thus one finds there the usual radical left side by side with the radical right. As radicalism is logically impossible, every version of it is tampered, and the same holds with a vengeance for the radical right. Thus the radical right in the United States is a mix of radicalism, especially in economics, and of conservatism, especially in matter of internal security. All this opens much room for debates that can be very exciting and fertile.

Chapter 11
Disputes About Aesthetics

Abstract In aesthetical debates, consider how much each view rests on shared psychology. Thus, an artefact is considered beautiful when it is seen as unexpected or surprising (non-trivial) yet as conforming to the rules of its own production, whatever these are. (These rules may serve as an item for an interesting preliminary discussion in the field of art appreciation).

This final chapter refers to aesthetic disputes. People argue about which sculptures to display in museums, which pictures to hang on walls of their home, what kind of (public) building to build and what dress fits what person best on this or that occasion. How can such disputes be resolved?

Let us repeat for the last time. Skeptical considerations lead to the conclusion that there is no way to measure the plausibility of aesthetic judgments. (Skepticism is presented in the Appendix below.) No aesthetic judgment is certain or plausible, skeptics say: there is no aesthetic knowledge, and no valid method exists for resolving aesthetic disputes. Some skeptics go further and say, there is no aesthetic objectivity. What they should say is, of course, possibly there is no aesthetic objectivity. But then they may say also, there is aesthetic objectivity. And so it is, as usual, the skeptic position that encourages disputes and debates. Some say, skepticism makes all disputes senseless, since they can never be settled with finality. This is unwise. First, an endless dispute may be enjoyable and profitable. (Skeptics who deny this are scarcely skeptics.) Second, skepticism permits settling disputes, even though not with finality, and this too may be enjoyable and profitable, since settling a dispute usually opens newer disputes, and these may be more challenging ones. If debates—on aesthetic questions or on any other questions—are progressive, then we can always look forward to newer and more challenging debates.

The idea that doubt hampers disputes leads to sad conclusions. Thus, in the field of aesthetics it leads too many people to say that beauty does not exist; hence, they consider an entire illusion the fact that we consider some things beautiful, or at least more beautiful that other things. The popular expression of their view is, beauty is in the eye of the beholder.

Not so. In particular, if aesthetic judgment were entirely arbitrary, it would be very strange that in so many cases, so many people agree about aesthetic issues of all sorts. Without such agreements there would be no museums and no concert halls and even no libraries and no top ten records. Aesthetic agreement, we suggest, is in part—but only in part—due to shared psychology. We propose to start with it as psychology is easier to discuss than metaphysics, you remember. For example, we appreciate beautiful things more if they are less frequent and so less commonplace. This is not necessarily so, since we may appreciate sunsets even if we see them every day. Nevertheless, even an exceptional sunset may be judged more beautiful than the average sunset, namely, unexpected, namely, not trivial. Obviously, scarcity is not a sufficient condition for beauty. Thus, babies look beautiful more often than adults do, even when they are seen frequently; moreover, small noses and ears are often perceived as more beautiful than big ones, perhaps because they resemble noses and ears of babies. Also, having red hair is infrequent and as such it is unexpected, but it is not considered beauty *per se*. It has been attested empirically that in a society with shaved men bearded ones look more handsome and vice versa. This, of course, is amusing, but not too impressive, since we take serious aesthetic judgments to be less ephemeral: we do not expect a museum guards reduce their esthetic judgments of the masterpieces they see regularly just because they are tired of seeing them. And conductors who begin to lose the sense of beauty of the works they regularly conduct know that this is a signal telling them to quit.

This may hold even for the new experience of any real work of art. No doubt, in its novelty, experiencing it may strong and unrepeatable, yet as the experience happens, the surprising element of the artwork has to give way to its details, and these have to fit each other to comprise a whole, and so, in a distinct sense, they should be quite unsurprising. It is indeed a part of the artistic experience, especially at the first time that the parts fit each other convincingly, whatever this may mean, so that the experience is of a novelty that becomes right and so not quite novel: it must be both fresh and not arbitrary. This is particularly obvious in detective novels, where the convention of the *genre* prevents arbitrariness and requires surprise: the surprising part or aspect of a good detective novel is enjoyable repeatedly, unlike the surprising element of a cheap whodunit that is rightly called a spoiler. The surprise within a good thriller that does not vanish is what makes it remarkable. In many classic detective novels (Dostoevsky's *Crime and Punishment*, for a conspicuous example), the author reveals the solution to the riddle right up in front and yet manages to keep the tension and surprise readers. Thus, when arguing about a particular work of art, to some extent we can try to explain its beauty by describing the way in which it exhibits such qualities that we assume are responsible for its aesthetic value.

Consider then some most noticeable disputes about modern art, such as ones concerning abstract paintings: do they qualify as art? In many cases of debates of this kind, the concern with the artistic value of abstract painting, in general or in the style of a specific artist or of a single canvas, the question of the presence or absence of the artistic experience is only a part of the discussion, since this is a matter of fact. Often people are incredulous: when *bona fide* art critics repeatedly report that a certain canvas moves them, people who are not moved by that canvas tend to assume that the art critics fool them—for fun or for gain—since they fail to experience anything particular and even to empathize with the critics who report different feelings. This inability to sympathize is already a better item for debate than the mere report about the experience itself. Thus, the staple argument against the view that the painting under dispute is a work of art is that any child could have drawn it. This claim, if true, deprives the work of any claim for uniqueness and thus of any surprise, let alone the surprise that a genuine artwork is supposed to create. This argument may come up in a debate about a specific work but it is quite general. It appears in specific discussions of specific artworks, especially in the plastic arts, but it applies to the whole genre, and to other arts in the *avant-garde* genres such as dada, including plays. *Waiting for Godot* by Samuel Beckett is a famous example: for most of it two characters have a very lame conversation that express their frustration about Godot's failure to come without giving the audience a clue as to who Godot is and why the two wait for him; the audience have no clue as to this, except for the name that may indicate that the expected personality is none other than the Good Lord. There is no clue, however, to help the audience decide whether this is the playwright intention or not. This frustrates many audiences and they deem it no quite a play but a kind of spoof. Some eminent critics find it exciting and some of them even complain that later in the play a third character appears on stage. This is not to say that there is agreement about art critics. Perhaps the most controversial movie is *Last Year at Marienbad*, directed by famous director Alain Resnais from a screenplay by leading novelist Alain Robbe-Grillet. Some critics find it dreamlike and exciting, others find it boring to tears. Although it is hard to imagine a child directing a movie, it is not unthinkable that a child wrote the screenplay, which the hostile critics may claim. This argument is not the only one that frustrated audiences can launch against *avant-garde* art. To stay with examples from movies, take one that seems more in tune with the convention of a style, such as the star-studded *Last Tango in Paris*, directed by notorious Bernardo Bertolucci. The movie had a *succes de scandal* and this raises a different controversial question: can a movie with pornographic scenes be a work of art? This apart, leading film critic Pauline Kael declared it a great work of art and others, including some of her ardent fans, consider it sheer trash.

    The difference in aesthetic intuitions regarding artworks, abstract and figurative alike, concerns the ability to perceive intricate patterns in it. Some do see patterns in these works, while others see in them nothing but chaos or nothing but dull repetitions of old clichés. Such differences may be addressed by discussing these patterns or alternatively by exposing them as scant and unsatisfactory. The discussion may, however, get more general, and center on the question, can an artwork comprising clichés and nothing else claim the standing of a serious work of art? Many art critics and historians of art declare this impossible and dismiss any work comprising clichés no art, especially the ones that are meant to make their consumers feel pleasure; they call them chocolate-box art. Can chocolate-box art count as art proper? Can operetta be art? Can people of good taste enjoy an evening at the operetta as an artistic experience? This question is existential, and so, you remember, invites those who assert existence to provide examples if they can. If they cannot, they may discuss a hypothetical artwork and even cause an artist to try it out, which comes to show how fruitful aesthetic debates can be. There are many contenders here. Some operettas of Offenbach or Johan Strauss. Some canvases of Toulouse Lautrec or Modiglianior the films of Charlie Chaplin or the famous *All about Eve* may count.

And then opponents may dismiss these as not clichés or as poor art. This kind of discussion will improve the ideas of participants in them concerning clichés and concerning art. It will obviously diverge into other debates, concerning such matters as the difference between clichés, *Kitsch*, and chocolate-box art, if there is any. We leave the elaboration of all this to our readers who are interested in art.

Without discussing this matter, we can consider a dispute about whether or not a certain painting is *kitsch*. The parties to the dispute can try to resolve it by considering whether the patterns in the object under consideration are only allegedly unexpected (and therefore hardly *kitsch*) or not. Moreover, some works of art combine items that are obviously *kitschy* in some new and surprising ways that may actually be aesthetically valuable. Indeed, famously, Picasso was eager to listen to aesthetic debates as a source of inspiration.

Simpler cases of valuable aesthetic criticism are the criticism of opinions of people who express inconsistent aesthetic judgments. A person may express enthusiasm regarding one piece of folksy music because it cites some genuine folk melodies and regarding another piece of folksy music because its folk melodies are all original. Drawing that person's attention to that inconsistency may lead to reconsideration and then perhaps a change of some aesthetic judgment. People, who express disdain for opera, explaining it as dislike for the artificiality of singing dialogues, may reconsider this in light of their toleration of the same artificiality in musical plays in light of the argument against naturalism in art. Of course, there is no objection to the appreciation of both abstract or *avant-garde* art and traditional or conventional art, or both highbrow and lowbrow art. If one wishes to account for these with an aesthetic theory, however, one has to avoid both the highbrow theory that rejects lowbrow art (as many aesthetic theories do) as well as the theory that rejects the avant-garde (such as socialist realism). It is very easy to be inconsistent. Thus, Bertold Brecht supported the Marxist view that good art must be progressive yet he (rightly) praised the famous 1939 adventure movie *GungaDin* that is decidedly imperialist.

This, let us observe, is not unusual. Notably, many people regularly express aesthetic judgments and present theories, thereby inviting debates about their consistency—or about other aspects of their pronouncements—or at least opening the door to debates. The commonest inconsistency is to claim that beauty is in the eye of the beholder and yet pronounce aesthetic judgments. Of course, one can say, I greatly enjoy some poor art (operetta or detective thrillers or science fiction), and perhaps offer some explanation; to say this is to deny that beauty is in the eye of the beholder, since the idea that beauty is in the eye of the beholder identifies beauty with the pleasurable experience of art. To appreciates some art without enjoying it—say, because it brings sad associations or because one feels tired or moody—is to distinguish between aesthetic value and the enjoyment of art. No doubt, art is for pleasure, but not all great pleasure is of good art.

Admittedly, the distinction between the aesthetic pleasure and the pleasure that a piece of art—any piece of art—may cause is psychological, but it is not only psychological. This is why aesthetic views are open to debates. And because debate about them is possible, they may cause changes of mind. This happens repeatedly when the disapproval with which a new artistic style or a new art form is first met with turns into approval. (Attitudes towards impressionism comprise a paradigm case of such a change.) Admittedly, some disputes about aesthetics are frustrating; but, remember, no kind of dispute and no topic of dispute is utterly free of frustration. Our aim in this handbook is to help you reduce the frustration of debates to a reasonable level and we repeatedly claim that the reluctance to enter disputes in order to avoid frustration causes a different kind of frustration— different but not a smaller —since some situations comprise strong temptations to engage in disputes. So we propose that rather than avoid arguing about aesthetics you may want to engage in preliminary discussions of the question, what will reduce the frustration. We have proposed here that the assertion that an artwork is unusual-yet-not-arbitrary may help. Obviously, other means are available, and interlocutors may air their views on this before engaging in the specific controversy that invites the debate and also discuss the question, what argument if any will make them admit error. Finally, as always, the best means for the reduction of frustration from debates is the benefit from them. Debating art and losing is the best means for developing one's taste and thus the experience of the joy of art. Particularly individuals who have no art in their educational backgrounds—those who have experienced hardly any art at home or in school—do hold ideas about art; airing them is the best known means for opening them up to the joy of artistic experience.

Chapter 12
Conclusion

Abstract Avoid frustrating debates. Avoid arguing with dogmatists and more so avoid arguing with relativists. Learn to enjoy and benefit from debates by recording your impressions from debates soon after they take place.

In contemporary society, finding argument painful is still popular. Thus, agreement is considered agreeable and disagreement disagreeable. This handbook advocates the opposite view. We claim that disputes can be fruitful and therefore enjoyable. We also claim that agreement is easier to achieve than disagreement, which is a well-known fact, masked by being called conformism. The most important aspect of disagreement is that to be fruitful it should be respectful. Contrary to received opinion, we assert that disagreement can be respectful. Participants in properly conducted disputes learn from it, and so we should naturally appreciate and respect those with whom we share the process of learning—through debates. Finally, we claim that the recognition of these facts may help change our misguided dislike for disagreement. Nevertheless, we agree with the general view that disputes can be frustrating; often, they are frustrating simply because most people engage in debates with no prior training, which renders their debates useless and thus frustrating.

Throughout this handbook, we have listed practical recommendations for the adoption of rules that help avoid frustrating debates and construct fruitful ones. In this concluding chapter, we will repeat our main practical recommendations.

First, make sure that the debating parties agree as to what is the question under dispute. The question should be worded as an interrogative sentence (one that begins with a question word and ends with a question mark). Questions with vague wording such as, "how about x, y or z?" are better not taken up. As every question rest on some presuppositions, it is advisable to spend some time on checking whether all parties to the dispute share the main presuppositions to the question under dispute. In any case, the parties to the dispute can agree to agree for the sake of the debate to assume these presuppositions. Alternatively, they should debate the questions that the disputed presuppositions answer. This procedure takes time, but in our opinion all of our proposals take time to implement but they save more time and reduce the level of frustration to a reasonable minimum.

Once the question under dispute and the presuppositions behind it are reasonably clearly stated and agreed upon, the debate can start. Notably, there is no need to worry whether this precondition has been sufficiently met or not: if the background information proves to not be adequately clear and the debate starts getting frustrating, then it is always possible to take a step back and discuss the background material a bit more before proceeding. We recommend doing so without fuss. Of course, it is advisable to avoid focusing so extensively on the background material that the issue at hand is never reached. (Such situations have happened to the best of us; one of the best known and most influential philosophy books ever, *Essay Concerning Human Understanding* by John Locke, is the product of a preliminary discussion.) To that end, list all the answers you can imagine to the question under dispute, reasonable and unreasonable, and then agree to delete from the list the answers that all parties to the dispute consider unreasonable. An answer is unreasonable if and only if no reasonable party will advocate it, of course.

Our next recommendation is simple as it is a recommendation for some avoidance of a pitfall. Do not debate definitions of concepts. Instead of trying to argue about the "right" definition of a certain concept, clarify its meaning by presenting examples, mainly paradigm cases. (If the concept is technical, its definition is not under dispute.) Remember: different definitions may be applicable; the result is synonymy, having one word with more than one meaning. This will not cause confusion if the parties to a dispute can always ascertain the right meaning of any problematic appearance of any word.

Pay attention as to who bears the burden of proof. Those who claim that their opponents are inconsistent should prove their claim (the opponents cannot prove that they are consistent), and those who claim that a certain generalization is false should point at cases that refute it (there is no way to prove that a factual generalization is true). Finally, when one side presents an existential statement (X exists) this side bears the burden of proof.

And here is another recommendation for some avoidance of a pitfall. Do not try to resolve disputes by measuring objectively the plausibility of the opinions under dispute. Strong skeptical considerations suggest that the plausibility of statements cannot be measured, let alone objectively, much less before the debate proceeds in earnest. (This is why debates are scarcely avoidable for those who seek intellectual improvement.)

When debating factual questions, it makes sense to consider whether each answer reduces the strangeness of the world, and perhaps also to what degree. Check which theory is simpler; when two theories explain the same phenomenon, we tend to endorse the simpler one. Check also whether the theory under dispute successfully predicts surprising facts that were not previously known or rather just explains known facts (the latter is easier than the former). Always prefer to debate the answer that seems to you easier to debate: difficult discussions are better postponed as much as reasonably possible. Following this advice will teach that it is reasonable to postpone complex discussions much more than it initially seems.

Avoid debates with partners who repeatedly change the formulation of their assertions whenever they encounter refutations by applying *ad hoc* corrections to them, especially if they pretend that these additions comprise clarifications rather than corrections. On the whole, prefer adversaries who admit to error frankly, preferably if they do so with no fuss.

When the assertion under dispute is an explanation of some phenomenon, investigate first the assertion that the phenomenon in question is due to a mere accident. And always consider whether it merits debate.

Avoid debates about causality (unless you are a philosopher). Usually, the interesting question under dispute involves the degree to which the appearance of one variable helps predict the appearance of another.

If the difference between two samples is statistically significant, you may still inquire whether this difference is interesting. Within large samples, even a small difference might be statistically significant yet not necessarily interesting or relevant to the concern that has prompted it.

When debating metaphysical questions, in many cases each of the views under dispute entails strange consequences. In such cases, arguing that a certain view cannot be true since it bears strange implications is not a valid argument, although it may convince advocates of the metaphysical idea at hand to reconsider their views.

Some views, mainly metaphysical, refer to claims about future events (for example: one day, it will be possible to construct conscious machines). In debates on such predictions, the contending parties are supposed to show that such events *in principle* cannot happen or alternately that they should happen as no principle prevents their occurrence. The parties to the dispute should agree on this; otherwise we propose to postpone the debate as it might be very frustrating.

Avoid arguments about whether some entity exists, unless you can agree in advance regarding manageable criteria for admitting or denying its existence. Indeed, such criteria may be subject to preliminary debates.

When debating whether a certain historical narrative is true, it makes sense to look for predictions implied by the hypothesis that it is (or is not) and then to research historical records in order to test these predictions. It might also be advisable to check whether the event under discussion could be expected under common general assumptions regarding human behavior. A similar recommendation holds regarding long-range predictions.

In debates about subjunctive conditional statements (answers to questions of the form "what would have happened if …?"), we recommend the investigation into the degree to which one event usually serves as means for predicting the other. Such investigation parallels that of the arguments about causality mentioned above.

When debating moral questions, it makes sense to consider the extent to which each view rests on sympathizing with the suffering of others versus the extent to which its adoption rests on the hope that acting on it will increase human welfare. Such understanding can help clarify some rather abstract notions that might otherwise disrupt such debates.

When debating aesthetical questions, consider how much each view rests on shared psychology. For example, in order for an artefact to be considered beautiful, it should be seen as unexpected or surprising (not trivial), yet as conforming to the rules of its own production, whatever these are (which may indeed serve as a good item for an interesting preliminary discussion that belongs to the field of art appreciation).

In general, pay attention to the difference between theories (that comprise general statements) and evidence (in the form of existential statements). In many disputes, mainly about technological, ethical, and political problems, the disputing parties may agree about the list of advantages and drawbacks of each of the possible options that the competing answers offer, but they may disagree about the benefits of these advantages and the cost of the disadvantages. In such cases, the disputes are not about theories, and it makes sense to concentrate on evaluating the costs and the benefits involved. Focus on what matters—what the parties to the dispute agree matters most; settle this important point before delving into the debate, if it is at all necessary: preliminaries to debates may and often do render them superfluous.

Avoid frustrating debates. Avoid arguing with dogmatists and more so avoid arguing with relativists. Such endeavors are assured to frustrate as they merely waste time and lead nowhere. Notably, relativists have one advantage over dogmatists: they announce themselves as relativists, whereas dogmatists usually deny that they are dogmatists. If a debate starts turning around in circles, you may suspect that one party is dogmatic. (It may be you! Just consider this as an option for a while before dismissing it.) It is worthwhile for all parties to a dispute to ask, "What will make you change your mind?" Astronomers would change their minds if one fixed star started moving freely on the sky-map, and biologists would change their minds if they had dug up layers of bones in the wrong evolutionary order. The belief in a miracle would fade out when someone reproduces the act in question at will. Of course, such examples are not good enough, as no one expects such things to happen (even if we can note some rare examples of such precious occurrences), but this is a good start, since such a discourse is anything but frustrating, and it shakes up the dogmatist in most of us. Remember, our main recommendation is that you learn that it is your right to enjoy a debate and that you insist on receiving the pleasure more-or-less at once. You will find that not only you yourself but also your partners to the debate will benefit from such insistence. Few involvements lead to good fun like productive, enlightening debates.

A word on public debates. In public debates the rules are different from the rules discussed here. The participants in them do not intend to learn and they address not their interlocutors but the public. This is incentive for rhetoric and even demagoguery. When you have to participate in a public debate find out the rules of the debate and learn something about the moderator, if you can. See that the rules are fair. If not, you must decide whether you want to participate. When your opponents use rhetoric, repeat what they say in plain words before you offer an alternative or criticism to it. The main thing to remember is that unlike private debates public debates need not be fun and they tend to frustrate. The frustration can be reduced by learning that it is unavoidable and by remembering why you undertook to partake in them in the first place.

Appendix: Skepticism

Throughout this book, we have referred to skepticism. This Appendix is a brief presentation of it. We find it necessary because regularly it appears in the literature as the pitfall to avoid as it is contrary to both science and commonsense; we present it throughout this handbook as the soul of both science and the commonsense of contemporary society.

From the beginning of philosophy, one of the main questions on its traditional agenda was (and to a large extent still is), how is it possible to prevent (or at least minimize) error while discovering interesting features of our world? Philosophers have been trying to present methods that ascertain that we endorse only information we know to be true, but all their suggested methods are refuted. Skepticism is the view that no such method exists, and even in principle. Most philosophers consider this a council of despair and we argue that on the contrary, it is the only philosophy that allows for hope and for some explanation of the facts of scientific progress.

Skeptics have raised two kinds of argument against the claim that certitude is attainable. One kind is specific arguments in various fields, such as skepticism in regard to perception, and the other kind is general. A statement is certain or justified if it is proved, but proof is impossible since theory about proof or any criterion for the validity of a proof requires a different proof for it. A justification procedure invites a justification for itself, and so on *ad infinitum*. Hence, final proof or justification is impossible. For example, character witnesses are possibly unreliable, and then for their testimony to be acceptable they need character witnesses to testify that they are reliable. But character witnesses need character witnesses to be credible. And so on, until we exhaust the population. (Indeed, when a mafia boss needs a character testimony, the entire population of the town are likely volunteers.)

This is not to say that there can be no true character witness. These do exist, and they are usually more reliable than the character witnesses for the mafia boss. Moreover, since proper testimonies are cross-examined, a good lawyer can make judge and jury ignore character testimonies for mafia bosses. The skeptic argues merely that such testimony is never certain. We usually agree that the skeptical argument is valid, but we tend to ignore it until and unless the skeptic brings some concrete evidence. For example, to say that the character witnesses who make the person in question look good may be pressured to testify is insufficient: we want evidence that they have indeed been pressured into doing so. Suppose a disaster happens and believers in the conspiracy theory say, some people benefit from this disaster and they have brought it about. This may always be true: we cannot rule out the possibility that some people somewhere are responsible for the disaster in question. To be taken seriously, however, this claim needs more details to support it. The best such detail is called a 'smoking gun': Tom has a gun directed towards Dick, the gun smokes and Dick falls dead with a bullet in his heart. We surmise that Tom has killed Dick. The terrific short story "The Man who Shot Liberty Valance" by Dorothy M. shows convincingly that this need not be so, but without further evidence we take it for granted that it is so, although only as the default option. We do take it for granted that some innocent people were executed after due process, that due process is no foolproof guarantee. This is why there is so much opposition to capital punishment. This shows that we are skeptics and deem skepticism commonsense.

What makes this commonsense across the board is that in modern society all people are in principle allowed to try to overturn any default options. We take it for granted that the specific details that make us take the odd option seriously comprise arguments against the default option: they are counter-examples against it; they refute presentations of allegedly reliable sources of knowledge. Thus, the skeptic arguments against each of the methods suggested for achieving knowledge separately and against all of them together does not overrule the default options together: it allows for overruling each of them separately.

In its strongest wording (to which we adhere), skepticism is the position that no statement is certain, plausible, justified, etc., in the sense that considering it erroneous is impossible under any condition. This is certitude in the epistemological sense of the word. The opponents to skepticism argued that this position is absurd since it leads to utter inaction, and indeed to total paralysis. For, the argument goes, the skeptics cannot choose what to believe. Not so, the skeptics answer. Psychological processes determine our beliefs.

Similar arguments are presented in regard to skepticism in ethics and aesthetics. It was claimed that skepticism in ethics leads to nihilism, but skeptics reject this argument by pointing to facts: most people hold some moral views yet are ready to discuss them. This can be fruitful. Similarly, skepticism in regard to aesthetical judgments does not lead to aesthetical nihilism, and people largely share aesthetical judgments. This is particularly intriguing in modern society that displays a great variety of art, since the proliferation of artworks requires the achievement of the existing consensus; this is often due to debates that are at times prolonged and even take generations to settle.

Finally, one way to dismiss skepticism is to endorse views and modes of action quite dogmatically. Some dogmatists admit frankly that they adopt a dogma so as to avoid skepticism. This choice is known as fideism. Although skeptics need not choose fideism, skepticism as such is not opposed to fideism: the arguments against it—and they are strong—do not arise from the skeptical arsenal.

In this handbook, we presented tentative theories regarding the psychological processes that help determine choices of opinions and of actions. Some of these processes are beneficial, we hope, and others may unfortunately be harmful. But all in all, it behooves us to admit that we do not know, since the admission of ignorance is the first step towards the search for any improvement. Of course, we may have no improvement, but thus far the search was fun, it seems, and it may be even more fun if you develop your ability to argue fruitfully and avoid frustration. And if your ability will develop far enough, you will be able to criticize and improve upon this handbook.

A Brief History of Skepticism

Socrates already presented himself as a skeptic. By raising questions, he undermined assertions that his peers considered obvious truths. He concluded that wisdom rests upon the awareness of ignorance. His most illustrious disciple was Plato, who founded the Academy and taught that knowledge can be founded on mathematics. After his death, the Academy returned to the Socratic tradition and was renowned for its skepticism. The philosophers who taught there practiced the method that Plato excelled in, the method of arguing for and against different answers to given questions, in suspense of all final judgments as to which answer is right.

The idea that the suspension of judgment is a virtue became the central teaching of Pyrrho and his followers, the Pyrrhonists. No written evidence attests to Pyrrho's position, but the prevalent view regarding it follows Sextus Empiricus who presents Pyrrhonism as follows. Those who wish to dwell in a peaceful temperament (*ataraxia*) should try to argue against every position that they tend to prefer: their view of any question should be as balanced as possible. As a result, they will refrain from assuming any position, and the outcome will be a permanent state of peace of mind. All this is nowadays almost entirely ignored.

Sixteenth-century European scholars, especially astronomers (Nicolaus Copernicus, Johannes Kepler, Galileo Galilei) discovered that disagreement is conducive to freedom of thought. Others discovered the writings of Sextus and found their arguments congenial. Conspicuous among them was Michel Montaigne. He used extant disagreements among scholars as evidence that science is as much a cultural construct as is religion, and proposed approaching it with much doubt. Erasmus of Rotterdam, who used skeptical arguments to attack Martin Luther's doctrine, claimed that we should conform to existing traditions, since there is no utterly reliable criterion of truth to apply in efforts to overthrow them, much less to replace them by better ones, except after long deliberations and experimentations that allow tradition to absorb the innovations.

Modern philosophy emerges in the beginning of the seventeenth century with the ideas of Francis Bacon and René Descartes, who advocated the dismissal of all past opinions without distinction so as to be able to start afresh and thereby achieve true knowledge. These two great fathers of modernity were concerned with science, and they intended to teach people to avoid error. They saw human beings as the source of all error and considered the source of all truth to be God or Nature; the choice between these options, they claimed, depends on one's view of the world. We may err when we speculate, they observed. So we should avoid speculation, they demanded.

David Hume is the philosopher who is mostly associated with skepticism in the eighteenth century, although he considered this a great injustice to himself, even an insult, since, as he noted, nothing is easier than the throwing of doubt in all directions indiscriminately. His moderate skepticism involved the recognition of the futility of Pyrrho's version of skepticism. He referred to two types of skeptical views: Pyrrhonism (which he rejected) and moderate skepticism (which he embraced), according to which, in spite of skeptical arguments, our psychology saves us from suspending all belief. Very much the way Descartes went about, Hume too first proved utter doubt and then offered a tool for escape there from it. But whereas Descartes' tool involved mathematics, Hume's involved psychology. He established doubt by arguing forcefully that all beliefs are doubtful except beliefs in immediate experiences. For, he argued, there is no rational principle that leads from the certainty of experience to any other certainty (or even probability) of belief in any idea about the world. Among the many skeptical arguments that Hume presented, the most famous one refers to induction: The fact that for eons the sun unfailingly rose every morning is no guarantee that it will rise tomorrow. Therefore, the statement asserting that it will remains in doubt.

Hume failed to convince his readers that his skepticism was moderate. Many of them saw him as a skeptic proper, as a Pyrrhonist; this remains and the dominant view of him, despite his touching protest, since he did boost the traditional Pyrrhonist arguments. This is regrettable, as he was of the opinion that certain *data* are certain, and so he obviously was not quite as much of a Pyrrhonist as his critics said he was.

In the nineteenth century irrationalism flourished, especially on German soil, and its adherents offered some bizarre metaphysical systems as expressions of their irrationalism and as means to undermine science proper. Rationalists could not bring themselves to admit that the irrationalist critique of rationalism had some value. So the rise of irrationalism regrettably pushed the excessive defenders of rationalism to the enhancement of the traditional hostility to metaphysics, and this hostility got a new name: positivism, to mean faith in reason and in science (to the exclusion of faith in any metaphysics). This was an excessive stress on the radicalism of traditional philosophy of science. It transformed rationalism into a kind of a political party, one that allied itself regularly with the radical political parties proper; loyalty to it made discussions of skepticism improper, since skepticism undermines science. This is an error: skepticism and positivism often coincide. Indeed, the name David Hume always invokes both together, perhaps because his hostility to metaphysics was brave and systematic. (His positivist ideas about religion appeared in print only posthumously even though they were politically correct.)

The great breakthrough arrived around the middle of the nineteenth century, in the same period as that in which positivism flourished: this was William Whewell's theory of scientific method as the method of empirical verification. He claimed that

Appendix: Skepticism

there is a way to defy the disposition to interpret observations as if they agree with our ideas: researchers develop a new idea, conclude from it that a special arrangement should give rise to certain new observations, and test this conclusion empirically. Since the source of new ideas is human imagination, they are not likely to be true. So test normally refutes them. So they try again and again. When a test comes up positive, it verifies the tested theory. This is how science progresses, he concluded.

This terrific theory did not appeal to philosophers because it makes the success of scientific research depend upon luck. Researchers, however, liked it very much, and for the very same reason. So philosophers forgot Wheel and the idea of verification. Researchers did remember it, but they forgot its originator. When Wheel's ideas were rediscovered, philosophers were less averse to the notion that research needs luck, and so the popularity of positivism increased. But the idea came too late: in the meanwhile, Albert Einstein caused a quiet revolution in philosophy. It was rightly in the shadow of his greater revolution in physics, but here it concerns us more: Einstein devastated the equation of error with sin that the scientific tradition unwittingly shared with Western religious traditions.

Under Einstein's influence, Karl Popper advocated *fallibilism*, the idea that any scientific theory may turn out to be false no matter how well it fits our experience to date. He joined Einstein in claiming that experience may either undermine theories or allow for them, but can never support them. Popper went further and claimed that to be scientific, even experience must be tentative. We take his argument even further, offering a form of skepticism that is slightly more radical. We follow him in advocating the idea that every informative statement is doubtful, never certain, plausible, corroborated, or justified—in the philosophical sense of these terms—and we include here even logic, especially since logic is the theory of rational criticism and this can hopefully improve (and thus render this handbook obsolete).

Bibliography

Agassi, Joseph. 1991. *The siblinghood of humanity: Introduction to philosophy*. Delmar: Caravan.
Agassi, Joseph. 1993. Conditions for interpersonal communication. *Methodology and Science* 26: 8–17.
Agassi, Joseph, and Abraham Meidan. 2008. *Philosophy from a skeptical perspective*. New York: Cambridge University Press.
Campbell, Tom. 2011. *Rights: A critical introduction*. London: Routledge.
Fitzpatrick, Mark. *High school debate rules & techniques*. http://www.ehow.com/info_8736679_debate-rules-techniques.html
Hume, David. 2000. *A treatise of human nature* (Edited by David Fate Norton and Mary J. Norton). Oxford/New York: Oxford University Press.
Patterson, Dennis. 1993. Psuedo-debate over default rules of contract law The symposium on default rules and contractual consent. *Southern California Interdisciplinary Law Journal,* 3. http://heinonline.org/HOL/Page?handle=hein.journals/scid3&div=17&g_sent=1&collection=journals#247
Plato. *Dialogues*, especially *Gorgias*, *Ion*. *Protagoras* and *Sophist*.
Popkin, Richard H. 2003. *The history of skepticism: From Savonarola to Bayle*, Revised edition. New York: Oxford University Press.
Popper, Karl. 2002a. *The poverty of historicism*, 2nd ed. New York: Harper & Row.
Popper, Karl. 2002b. *Conjectures and refutations: The growth of scientific knowledge*, 2nd ed. New York: Routledge.
Raney, Abigail. *How culture & society politics US politics rules of debate*. http://www.ehow.com/about_5283163_rules-debate.html
Roger, Michelle. 2010, January. *Reforming federal election debates in Canada, Centre for the Study of Democracy.* http://dspace.africaportal.org/jspui/bitstream/123456789/27527/1/Reforming%20federal%20election%20debates%20in%20Canada.pdf?1
Rosenburg, Amanda. *Does format matter? An analysis of the 2008 Presidential debates*. http://udspace.udel.edu/handle/19716/5503
Russell, Bertrand. 2004. *Skeptical essays*, 2nd edn. New York: W.W. Norton.
The debate: A report by the New York City Campaign Finance Board; June 1994. http://www.nyc-cfb.info/PDF/issue_reports/1994-06.PDF
Walton, Douglas. 2003. *Methods of argumentation*. Cambridge: Cambridge University Press (2013).

Index

A
Abortion, 105
Ad hoc theory, 47
Aerodynamics, 97
Aesthetics, 117
Age of Reason, 8
Amnesty International, 111
Animal rights, 103
Aristotle, 22, 55, 70, 83
Associationism, 74
Auschwitz, 80
Authenticity, 107
Avant-garde art, 119

B
Bacon, Francis, 20
Beckett, Samuel, 119
Berkley, George, 73
Bernoulli's law, 54, 65
Bertolucci, Bernardo, 119
Bible code, 53
Big Bang, 89
Blish, James, 7
Bohr, Niels, 78
Boyle, Robert, 80
Brainwashing, 25
Brecht, Bertold, 120
Broad, Charlie, 73
Buber, Martin, 81

C
Cabbalists, 115
Carnap, Rudolf, 17
Causality, 61, 87
Chaplin, Charlie, 119
Characteristica Universalis, 115
Charity, 103
Child abuse, 106
China, 12
Chinese room argument, 74
Clitorectomy, 108
Communism, 11
Competence *vs.* performance, 24, 31
Consciousness, 73
Conservatism, 110, 114
Conspiracy theories, 53
Controlled experiment, 62
Court procedures, 14, 40

D
Darwin, Charles, 50, 55
Darwin, Erasmus, 55
Darwinism, 29, 80
Definition, 38
Democracy, 11
Descartes, Rene, 72, 73
Determinism, 75
Dialectics, 23
Dictatorship, 11
Diminishing marginal utility, 109
Dirac, Paul, 50
Dogmatism, 19, 50
Dostoevsky, Fyodor, 118
Drugs, 85
  abuse, 33
Dual aspects theory, 73

E
Edison, Thomas Alva, 21
Einstein, Albert, 50, 52, 60, 72, 113
Electrical cars, 98
Eliot, George, 37
Encyclopedia Britannica, 71
Epiphenomenalism, 73
Esperanto, 115
Essence, 70
Ethics, 102
European Union, 113
Existence of God, 78
Existentialism, 107
Existential proposition, 36
Extrapolation, 51, 90

F
False negative/positive, 94
Fascism, 11
Fatalism, 76
Female circumcision, 108
Forecast, 89
Free choice, 75
Frege, Gottlob, 115
Freud, Sigmund, 5, 87, 88

G
Galileo, Galilei, 76
Gambler's fallacy, 54
Generalization, 36, 59
Genetically modified foods, 98
Gestalt school, 74
Giffen, Robert, 49
Global famine, 92
Global warming, 57, 99
God, 78
Gödel, Kurt, 79
Goffman, Erving, 87
Greek Philosophy, 10

H
Healthy diet, 67
Hegel, Friedrich, 39
Heine, Heinrich, 80
Hempel, Carl, 60
Heredity *vs.* environment, 34
Herodotus, 2
Hilbert, David, 115
Hiroshima, 80, 85, 89
Historicism, 90

History, 84, 85
Homosexuality, 107
Human rights, 110
Hume, David, 60, 61, 70, 103
Huxley, Thomas, 73
Hydrodynamics, 97

I
Idealism, 73
Immortality, 73
Impressionism, 121
Indeterminism, 75
Inequality, 111
Intelligent design, 82
Interactionism, 73
Interviews, 40

J
Japan, 12
Jarvie, Ian, 116

K
Kael, Pauline, 119
Kahneman, Daniel, 48
Kant, Immanuel, 69
Karamazov, Ivan, 80
Kennedy assassination, 86
Kepler, Johannes, 29
Kitsch, 120

L
La Mettrie, Julien, 73
Lancaster, Kelvin, 44
Laplace, Pierre-Simon, 17, 54, 76
Lautrec, Toulouse, 119
Lavoisier, Antoine, 51
Leibniz Gottfried, 73, 115
Lenin, Vladimir, 90
Liberalism, 116
Lifestyle, 101
Lipsey, Richard, 44
Lorenz, Conrad, 29
Lyell, Charles, 55

M
Machiavell, Niccolo, 116
Maimonides, Moses, 76, 81, 87
Male and female differences, 33

Malthus, Thomas, 92
Marshal, Alfred, 49
Marx, Karl, 39, 88, 90
Maslow, Abraham, 28
Materialism, 73
McCarthy, Joseph, 31
Meaning, 38
Medicine, 93
Mendel, Gregor, 50
Mendeleev, Dmitri, 78
Meritocracy, 116
Metaphysics, 69
Mind-body problem, 71
Modern art, 118
Modigliani, Amedeo, 119
Monarchism, 110
Monogamy, 35
Moral relativism, 108
Moscow show trials, 87

N
Nagasaki, 85
National rights, 112
Neutral monism, 73
Newton, Isaac, 49, 75
Non-government organizations, 104

O
Occam's razor, 51
Oedipus complex, 87, 88
Offenbach, Jacques, 119
Offspring responsibility, 107
Opportunity cost, 28

P
Paradigm cases, 38
Parallelism, 73
Pasteur, Louis, 46
Peano, Giuseppe, 115
Phlogiston, 51
Physico-theological argument, 80
Picasso, Pablo, 120
Plato, 2, 18, 22, 23, 79, 85
Plausibility, 16
Poincaré, Henri, 90
Politics, 102
Popper, Karl, 51, 52, 60, 69, 79, 88, 90, 110
Postmodernism, 18
Prediction, 65, 67
　　vs. explanations, 52

Presuppositions, 33
Priestley, Joseph, 52
Primitivism, 107
Psychoanalysis, 88

Q
Quora.com, 34

R
Racism, 29
Radicalism, 115
Raegan, Ronald, 104
Reductionism, 72
Refutation, 45
Relativism, 18, 19, 22
Resnais, Alain, 119
Revenge, 106
Rhetoric, 21
Robbe-Grillet, Alain, 119
Russell, Bertrand, 4, 20, 70–72, 79, 113, 115

S
Second best theorem, 43
Sexual freedom, 105
Shaw, Bernard, 18, 35
Simplicity, 50
Skepticism, 102, 117
Socrates, 39, 85, 102
Sophism, 18
Sophists, 10
Space-shuttles, 99
Spinoza, Benedict, 73, 76, 116
Stahl, Georg Ernst, 51
Statistics, 34, 59
Stone, Oliver, 87
Strangeness of the world, 46
Strauss, Johan, 119
Subjunctive conditionals, 84, 85, 88
Substance, 72
Sympathy, 103

T
Talmud, 12
Tax, 109
Technology, 93
Teicholz, Nina, 67
Thales, 83
Tversky, Amos, 48

U
Utility, 97
Utopia, 115

W
Welfare, 97, 103
Whitehead, Alfred, 115
Wilson, Woodrow, 112
Wittgenstein, Ludwig, 17–19, 69–71, 79

Wolfenden, John, 107
World government, 113
Wright brothers, 7
Würzburg school, 74

Z
Zamenhof, Ludwik, 115
Zuckmayer, Carl, 84

GPSR Compliance

The European Union's (EU) General Product Safety Regulation (GPSR) is a set of rules that requires consumer products to be safe and our obligations to ensure this.

If you have any concerns about our products, you can contact us on

ProductSafety@springernature.com

In case Publisher is established outside the EU, the EU authorized representative is:

Springer Nature Customer Service Center GmbH
Europaplatz 3
69115 Heidelberg, Germany